Decorating Furniture

Stencil, Paint and Block Print Projects

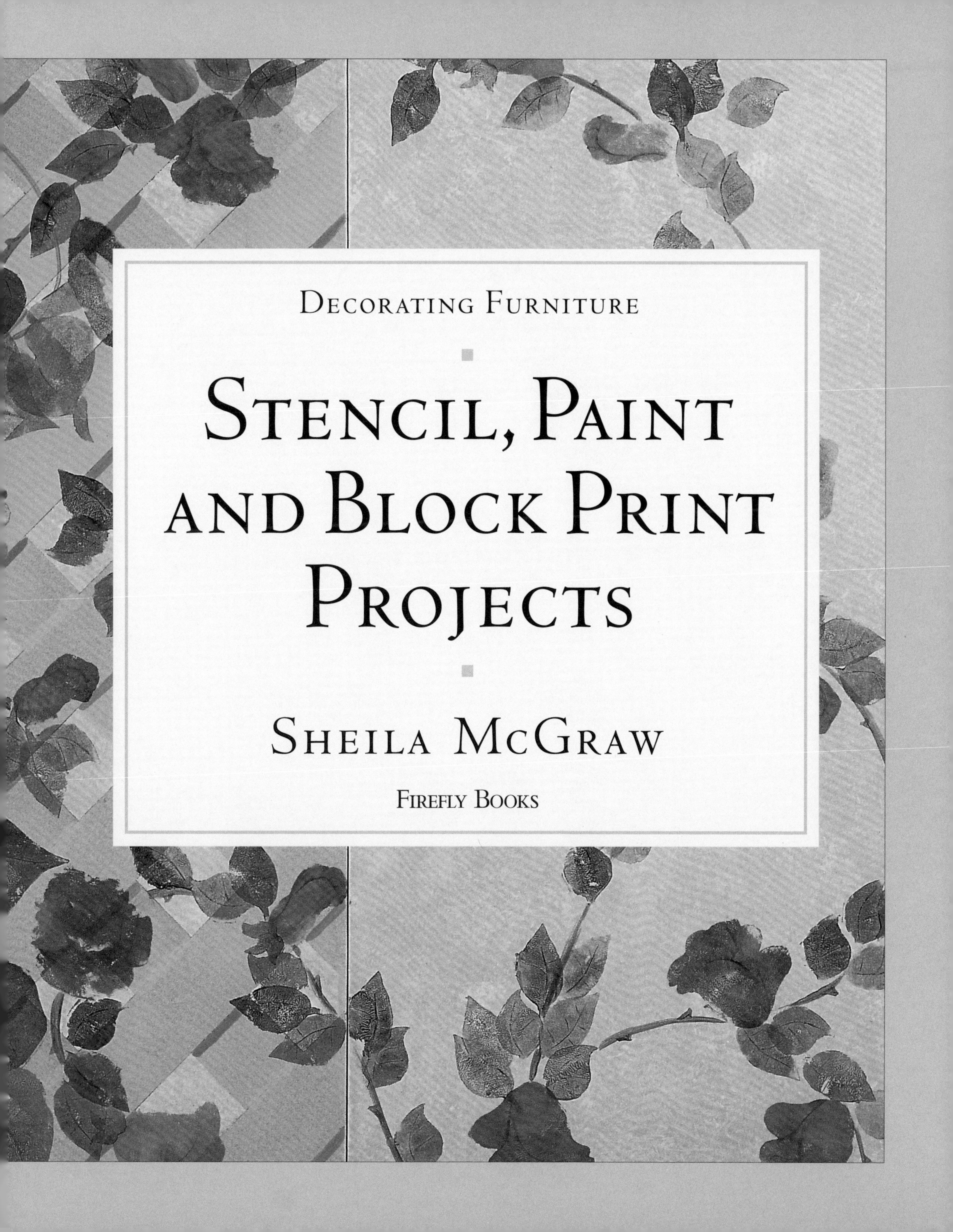

Decorating Furniture

Stencil, Paint and Block Print Projects

Sheila McGraw

Firefly Books

Published by Firefly Books Ltd. 2002
Copyright © 2002 by Sheila McGraw

All rights reserved. No part of this publication may be reproduced or transmitted in any form or by any means, electronic or mechanical, including photocopy, recording, or any information storage and retrieval system, without the written permission of the publisher.

National Library of Canada Cataloguing in Publication Data

McGraw, Sheila
Stencil, paint and block print projects / Sheila McGraw.

(Decorating furniture)
ISBN 1-55297-617-3

1. Furniture painting. 2. Decoration and ornament, Rustic. 3. Stencil work. I. Title. II. Series.

TT199.4.M338 2002 745.7 C2002-901442-5

Publisher Cataloging-in-Publication Data (U.S.)

McGraw, Sheila.
Decorating furniture : stencil, paint and block print projects / Sheila McGraw.—1st ed.
[128] p. : col. photos. ; cm. (Decorating furniture)
Summary: A step-by-step guide to furniture finishes including tools and materials, processes and projects.
ISBN 1-55297-617-3 (pbk.)
1. Furniture finishing. 2. Furniture painting. 3. Decoration and ornament. I. Title. II. Series.
745.7/ 23 21 CIP TT199.4.T34 2002

Text by Sheila McGraw
Photography and cartoon illustrations by Sheila McGraw
Design by Sheila McGraw and Counterpunch/Linda Gustafson
Page production by Counterpunch

Published by
Firefly Books Ltd.
3680 Victoria Park Avenue
Willowdale, Ontario
Canada M2H 3K1

Published in the U.S. by
Firefly Books (U.S.) Inc.
P.O. Box 1338, Ellicott Station
Buffalo, New York 14205 USA

Printed and bound in Canada by Friesens
Altona, Manitoba

The Publisher acknowledges the financial support of the Government of Canada through the Book Publishing Industry Development Program for its publishing activities.

Paints, chemical compounds and tools (manual or power), and any other materials suggested in this book, must be handled with care. Ventilation, and protective clothing and equipment, must be used wherever necessary. The author and publisher assume no liability for accidents, mishaps or allergic reactions that may arise from the handling of materials; or from moving furniture when painting and decorating furniture; or from the subsequent use of the furniture treatments shown in this book. To achieve the results shown, all steps and advice accompanying the project must be followed in the correct order, using the recommended materials. The author and publisher assume no liability for unsatisfactory workmanship.

To my son James

Acknowledgments

Thank you to everyone who worked with me on this book: Lionel Koffler for making the book possible; Pamela Anthony, Melanie Siegel and Pauline McGraw-Pike for their assistance, and for lending their hands for photography. Also to Max Piersig and Jason Wing for their strong backs and sharp minds. Thank you to all who lent their furniture to this project and let me go to town on it, and to those who opened their homes to me for photography. Special thanks to The Paint Depot in Toronto for their excellent advice, their cheerful enthusiasm and their patience. Thanks to designer Linda Gustafson for gleefully knocking heads with me to get it all on paper, and to my editors, Sarah Swartz and Dan Liebman. My appreciation to all the people who work behind the scenes producing and printing this book and to the staff at Firefly Books.

CONTENTS

Introduction

8

A Brush with Destiny 10
Using This Book 11
Choosing Your Furniture 12

Tools and Materials

14

Adhesives 16
Deglossing Agents 18
Manual and Power Tools 20
Metallics 22
Painting Tools 24
Paint Products 26
Paint Removers 30
Specialty Products 32

Painting Basics

34

Preparation 36
Priming and Painting 38
Brush Painting 40
Roller Painting 42
Spray Painting 44
Staining Wood 46
Varnishing 48

Projects

50

Rustic Recipes 50
Crackle with a Side Order of Potato Print

Prints Charming 56
Fluid, Fast Block Printing Adds Bedside Appeal

Lasting Impressions 62
A Simple, Striking School of Block-Printed Fish

Vanity Flair 68
Give Them the Moon and the Stars with Unique Reverse-Stencils

Ivy League 74
Set an Amber-Stained Table with Ivy Trimmed in Copper

Image Makers 80
More Intricate than Stencils, Transferred Designs Complement Personal Prose

Pretty Fantastic 86
Misty Rose Stencils Bedeck a Wooden Table

Sheer Delight 92
Gauzy, Printed Floral Vines Entwine Over Painted Trellis

Times Tables 100
Simple Stenciling Creates a Timely Classic

Art in Craft 106
Stenciled Copper Leaf Offsets Color and Crafted Copper

Seating 112
Sitting Pretty with Professionally Crafted Cushions and Seats
Basic Seat Cushion 115
Piped Seat Cushion 118
Woven Seat 121
Backrest Cushions 124

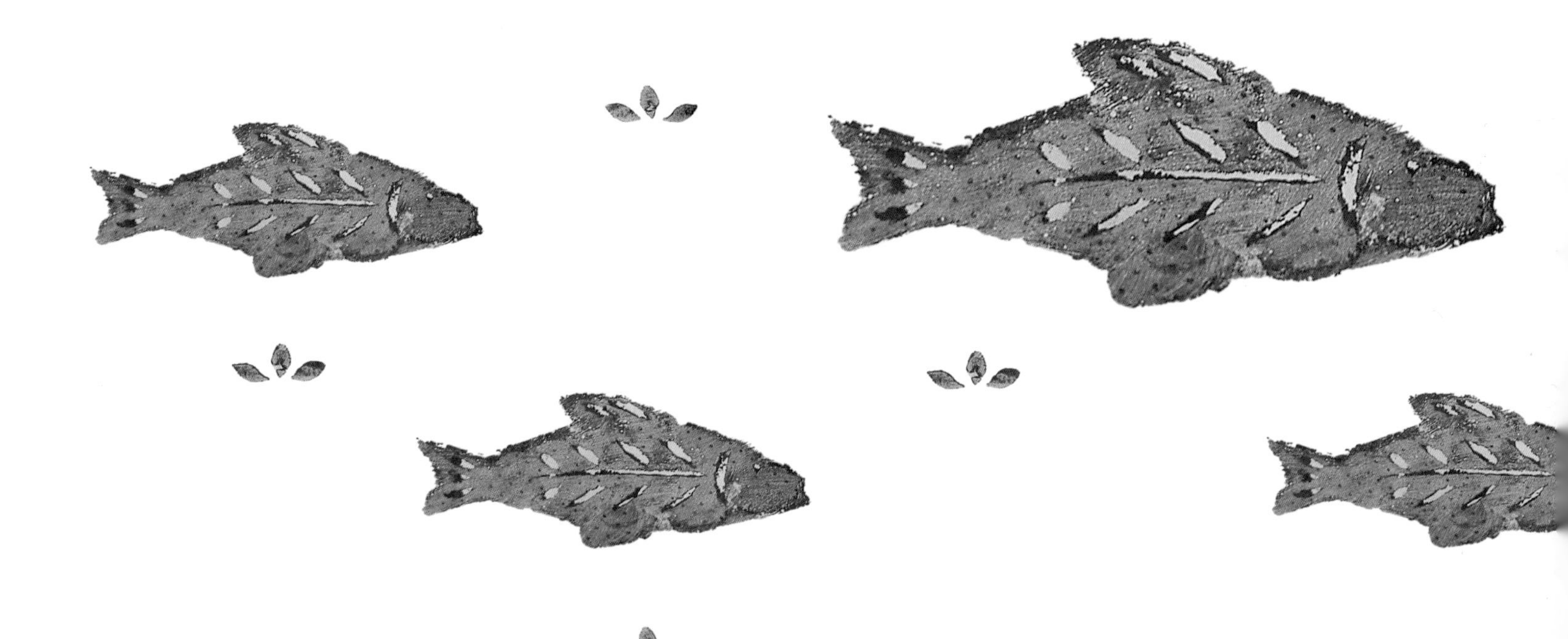

Introduction

This book is precisely the right prescription to get you out of your stenciling rut. It features exciting new ways to combine block printing and stenciling with other techniques, including freehand painting, textured backgrounds and even ornamental copper cut-outs. We show you block printing with a roller for borders or vine effects; how to make your own block prints; potato block-printing for a rustic look; and how to use block printing on both a painted and a stained background. And just when you think there is nothing left to learn about stenciling, we show three new techniques: stenciling metallic leaf, free-form stenciling and reverse-stenciling. If you have never stenciled or block printed, don't worry. The basics are laid out in a straightforward, easy-to-understand format. Also featured: a wealth of information and step-by-step instructions showing the materials, the paints, the background treatments and the techniques you need for inspired and functional art on your furniture.

A Brush with Destiny

Many a furniture painter sets out with the simple intention of slapping a fresh coat of paint over a time-worn piece of furniture, only to have inspiration strike. The surprise result is a beautifully hand-painted work of art, a family heirloom to be cherished for generations. The flat planes of furniture – tabletops, drawer fronts and the like – present endless opportunities for decorative and pictorial techniques, while the three-dimensional form is sculptural in nature, offering many angles for viewing. Painting and decorating furniture is creativity in the round. Often the busy grain of wood, an unsuitable finish, or simply the familiarity of a piece of furniture can obscure these qualities until you stand before it, paint and brush in hand.

If you feel indecision creeping up as you try to decide on the right treatment, determine which type of decorator you are.

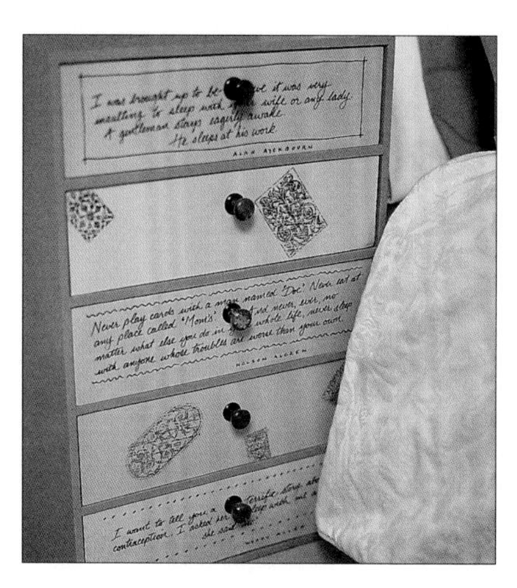

If you prefer furniture to be outstanding without standing out, think in terms of soft pastels or neutral colors and understated, tone-on-tone textures and treatments.

If you embrace the attitude that anything worth doing is worth overdoing, consider strong color, over-the-top decorative embellishments or a mixture of treatments for a grand statement.

It's no longer necessary to use slow-drying oil-based paints to achieve professional results.

Using This Book

Whether you are new to stenciling and block printing, or are highly skilled in the craft, this book will show you clearly and concisely everything you need to know. Beginners are shown the basics, including how to make stencils and block prints, which paints to use for which effects, and effective methods of application, while the advanced crafter will revel in innovative, never-before-seen techniques. This book is much more than a simple instructional guide; we have compiled a wealth of information to lead you through the maze of paints and tools available and show you how to manipulate and combine materials and techniques for wonderfully creative results. Check the *Tools and Materials* section (page 14), to acquaint yourself with the many easy-to-find and easy-to-use materials available at paint, craft and art supply stores. Unless absolutely unavoidable, only low-toxicity, water-based products are used and recommended. Water-based paints have evolved into easy-clean-up, simple-to-use, durable products.

Reading through the instructions before starting a project is like examining a road map. It helps you anticipate what's around the corner.

Painting basics such as brush painting, roller painting, spray painting, staining wood and varnishing are covered, as is performing a basic paint job for those who simply wish to paint their furniture a solid color. You'll also be referred by your project instructions to these sections as required. They provide a goldmine of basic, common-sense advice and time-saving tips.

To choose a treatment for your piece, flip through the book to find ideas that appeal to you, keeping in mind that the finished look should complement your furniture and that the projects are in a progressive order of complexity, starting with the simplest and becoming more involved as you go through the book. These advanced projects are not necessarily more difficult; they may simply require more steps, drying times or tools.

Measurements are listed in imperial units, with metric conversions following them. To make the instructions less cumbersome, the conversions are often rounded. A quart-sized can of paint is listed as a litre, for example; a yard is converted to a metre. The projects work whether you use the imperial or the metric measurements. Finally, don't let the toy penguin who appears in the *Before* pictures throw you. This little fellow is working for scale, providing a point of reference. Without him, the size of a cabinet or some other piece of furniture could be hard to judge from the photo.

The toy penguin who appears in the Before pictures is there to provide scale, and is 9 inches (22.5 cm) tall.

Test all moving parts of the furniture.

Choosing Your Furniture

Perhaps Aunt Flossie left you a four-legged monster. It's probably a sturdy, well-built, solid piece of furniture – better quality than you can purchase today. And it's free. Instead of relegating the monster to landfill, transform it to suit your decor and get ten or possibly a hundred years of use from it. If you don't have an Aunt Flossie, garage sales and flea markets are often treasure troves of old furniture. Another possibility is unpainted furniture – especially the knockdown variety, which is ideal for painting or staining in multiple colors. And don't throw out that plastic laminate furniture. Even recently manufactured melamine-over-chipboard furniture can be transformed with specialty melamine paints.

Just as the world is divided into cat lovers and dog lovers, it is also divided into furniture painters and furniture refinishers. Refinishers feel that wood and its grain are sacred, and that every stick should be stripped and refinished. Painters, meanwhile, believe that wood is simply nature's plastic, to be transformed into painted masterpieces. The truth is somewhere in between, and this book should help balance the two points of view. Virtually any style, type and finish of furniture can be painted, including wood, metal, melamine and all previously painted, lacquered and varnished pieces. But please: don't paint over genuine antiques or other pieces that have historic or architectural integrity, including classics from as recently as the 1960s and 70s. If you suspect your furniture has value, have it appraised. Often, you can simply take or send a snapshot to an appraiser or an auction house. If it turns out that you own a classic, but the style is unappealing to you, sell the item rather than paint it. Antiques with original paint should be left intact. Original paint on an antique, no matter how worn, adds to its authenticity and value.

If you wish to cut down on preparation time, look for a well-proportioned piece that is solid and has a stable finish. Beware of furniture with worm holes, especially if you see sawdust on the floor around the piece – a sure sign of bugs. When they move in, these boring guests will literally eat you out of house and home. And while you can't expect perfection – the furniture is

Interesting lines and curves can be accentuated to advantage in refinishing.

Even a piece this severely damaged has renovation potential.

Simply constructed wooden desks suggest antique, Victorian or rustic treatments.

supposed to be old and worn – try out all moving parts to determine the aggravation factor of drawers that bind or doors that stick, especially if the vendor has them taped shut. Remove drawers to check that dovetailing is intact and that the bottoms don't sag. If chairs or tables have wobbly legs, check that they can be fixed. Bypass the item if the legs have already had surgery but are wobbling a second time.

If you are planning to apply a smooth high-gloss treatment, choose a piece with a solid, even finish in good condition. Try the fingernail test. Scratching with your fingernail should not lift the finish. Pieces with dents, scratches, cigarette burns and water or other surface damage require a busy-looking, low-luster finish to distract from the imperfections. You may wish to steer clear of pieces with water damage that has lifted veneer. Loose or raised veneer must be removed and the scars repaired, a job that requires some skill. And take a tape measure to be sure the piece fits its final destination and can be maneuvered through doors and up stairwells.

1960s vintage furniture often features flat, smooth sides and fronts, ideal for stenciling and block printing.

When choosing a treatment, look for finishes that will enhance the intrinsic style and accentuate the lines of the piece.

If good design is form following function, then great style is the perfect adornment of good design.

Choose a finish in harmony with the mood of the furniture: rustic finishes for simple planklike constructions, Victorian treatments for decorative pieces, and glossy subdued finishes for simple modern furniture.

12 LOOMIS & TOLES CONSEIL 990F ENGLAND
8 LOOMIS & TOLES CONSEIL 990F ENGLAND

TOOLS AND MATERIALS

This section explains the properties and functions of the tools and materials used most frequently on furniture, from basecoat through decorative finishes. The stencil and block-print patterns, special paints and related materials needed for a particular application are discussed in the project in which they are required; for example, information on printing with potato prints is covered in *Rustic Recipes,* beginning on page 50. If several years have gone by since your last excursion to purchase paint, you are in for a pleasant surprise. Advancements in the technology of water-based paint have led to long-wearing products with low odor, smooth texture, a huge color range, dense coverage and fast drying times. Brushes, rollers, sandpapers and many other tools and materials for applying these paints have been redesigned to keep pace. And alongside the paints and brushes, you'll find innovative supplies, kits and other materials for a huge range of treatments.

Adhesives

Sticky Situations Call For Gentle Tapes, Supertacky Glues And Dependable Pastes

Glue White carpenter's glue dries clear and is extremely strong. Use white carpenter's glue for bonding wood when joining or repairing pieces of wooden or painted furniture. Apply a generous amount to the join and connect the two pieces. (If repairing a piece, first clean out the join with a utility knife or sandpaper before gluing.) Wipe away excess glue and clamp the pieces tightly overnight, cushioning the clamps if necessary to prevent them from denting the furniture. If clamps aren't available, bungy cords can often be tightly wrapped around the pieces. When staining a piece of furniture, stain pieces before gluing, since the glue can act as a sealer on the wood, resisting the stain.

Hot Glue With its fast drying time and good holding ability, a hot-glue gun is ideal for tacking decorative crafts. On furniture, it can be used for adding decorative detail or for finishing, but is not strong enough for gluing structural pieces of furniture. *When using a hot-glue gun, be careful.* This glue sticks to skin and can produce nasty burns. Some glue guns do produce a lower heat, but also a weaker tack.

Mucilage Mucilage is the amber-colored glue used in grade school. It comes in a slim bottle with a rubber nipple on top. Mucilage is the inexpensive magic ingredient used for creating crackled paint – the type that looks like flaking paint. The mucilage is painted onto a dry base coat of paint. While the glue is still wet, another color of paint is brushed over the glue. The different drying times of the glue and paint create the technique called crackle, which works best with latex paint. (See *Rustic Recipes,* page 50.)

TAPE Isolating areas to be painted by taping around them is called "masking." Ironically, masking tape is not a good choice of tape for this purpose. Easy-release tape, available in a light and medium tackiness, has two major benefits over masking tape. Easy-release tape is smooth and gives a crisp edge; masking tape tends to be slightly crinkly, permitting paint to ooze under its edge. Easy-release tape peels off most surfaces without disturbing the underlying finish, while masking tape often lifts paint. The only drawback of easy-release tape is its tendency to live up to its name by spontaneously falling off. The trick is to use small pieces of masking tape to tack the ends in place. Remove all tape as soon as possible after painting, preferably as soon as paint is dry to the touch. Any tape left on for long periods will leave gummy deposits or will fuse to underlying paint, tearing it off when the tape is removed.

(1) easy-release painter's tape; (2) masking tape; (3) white carpenter's glue; (4) mucilage; (5) C-clamps; (6) hot-glue gun; (7) cellulose wallpaper paste.

WALLPAPER PASTE Clear-drying, easy-to-work-with water-based wallpaper paste is the adhesive of choice for mounting large flexible materials, such as paper and fabric, to furniture. Purchase cellulose-based paste in dry form from your paint store and mix the required amount with water. This paste needs to sit for fifteen minutes or more after mixing (stir occasionally) for the granules to dissolve. Begin using the paste when it is a glutinous consistency. Use a large soft brush or a sponge to coat large pieces of paper or fabric, and use your hands to coat smaller surfaces such as découpage cut-outs and leaves. Wet pasted paper often develops wrinkles. These will shrink and disappear as the paste dries. Paper can also stretch and will then require trimming when it has dried.

SPRAY GLUE Available at hardware, paint, office supply, craft and art supply stores, this relatively new product is versatile and fast and offers a choice of temporary or permanent bond. Apply spray glue to the backs of stencils to make a light, long-lasting tack for holding the stencil in position. Spray glue can be used as a permanent adhesive for mounting fabric and posters, although it allows only one attempt at positioning. If this prospect causes anxiety, use wallpaper paste. In upholstery work, use spray glue for laminating foam to plywood, and batting to foam. Spray glue is also used for gluing block prints to a roller for continuous-printing jobs. The down side of spray glue? The overspray you get, and the amount of glue that sticks to your fingers.

When using spray glue, be careful to avoid becoming stuck on your project. This glue is tenacious. It sticks like, well, glue!

Deglossing Agents

New Sandpapers and Sandpaper Substitutes Make Deglossing Quicker and Cleaner Than Ever

Compounds Furniture with a lustrous finish must be deglossed before being painted, to ensure that the paint will adhere to the surface of the furniture. Very high-gloss or melamine finishes require a light sanding, but furniture that has a stable, non-flaking, low- or medium-luster finish can be deglossed with liquid deglossing agents. TSP or another liquid sandpaper can be used to dull the gloss and remove all grease and dirt. Mix the TSP with water according to the package label. Then, wearing rubber gloves, wash the piece with the solution and rinse well with clean water. Allow to dry overnight before painting.

Sandpaper To promote the best adhesion possible between the furniture's surface and the primer or paint, lightly sand surface areas that will be getting a lot of wear, using fine sandpaper (220 grade). High-gloss or plastic laminate finishes must be lightly sanded. This is a fast job. Remember, you're only deglossing the surface, not sanding down to bare wood. Sand the surface evenly until it has a dull surface texture. When sanding raw wood, always sand *with* the grain. Sanding lightly across the grain can leave deep permanent scratches. Sanding between coats of paint with fine sandpaper (220 grade or finer) will give a smoother, lacquerlike

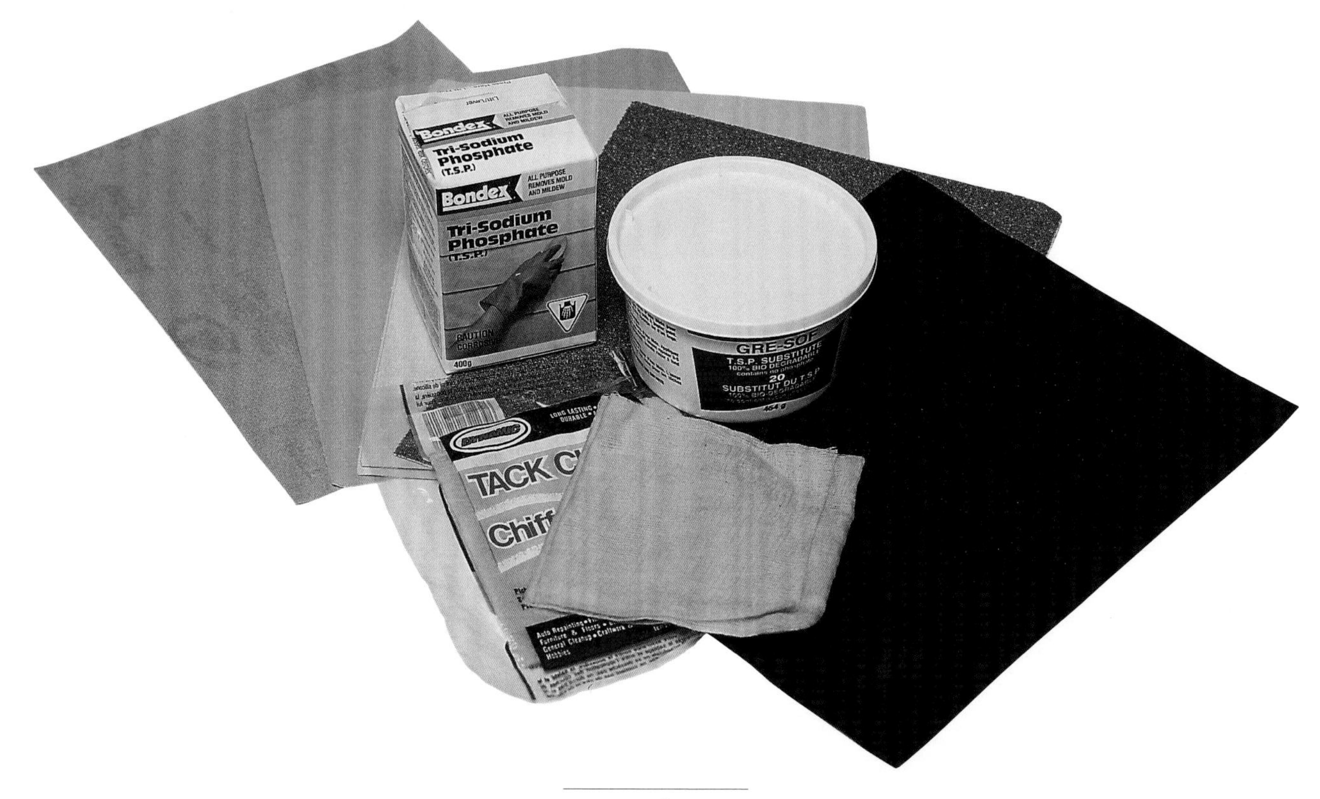

top coat. When varnishing, sand lightly with fine sandpaper (220 grade or finer) between coats. Don't be alarmed by the cloudy effect the sanding has on the varnish. The next coat will be smooth and clear. After sanding any surface, wipe away every trace of dust with a tack cloth.

Choose the right sandpaper for the job. The grit or grade, printed on the back, indicates grains of sand to the inch. The lower the number, the coarser the texture.

EMERY CLOTH Emery cloth – black sandpaper with cloth backing, and gray-black sandpaper with green paper backing – is produced only in very fine grades. Both varieties can be used wet for sanding metal or dry for wood and metal.

GARNET PAPER Brown in color, garnet paper is the most commonly used sandpaper. Use garnet paper for sanding wood, painted surfaces or plastic laminates. Available in very coarse to very fine grades, it is ideal for virtually all sanding requirements, except for sanding metal.

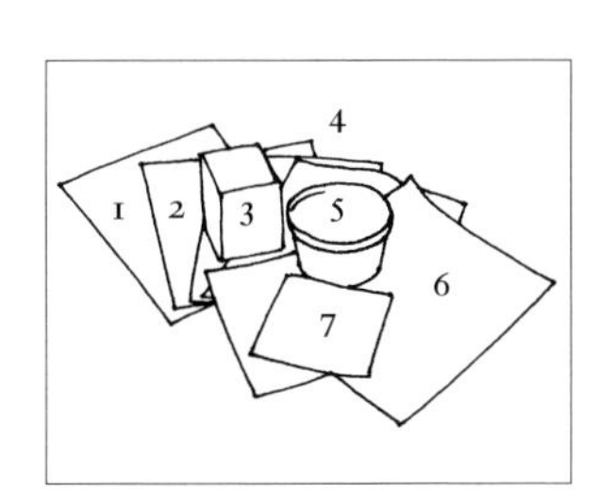

(1) fine garnet paper; (2) sandpaper for latex paint; (3) TSP deglossing compound; (4) coarse garnet paper; (5) biodegradable deglossing compound; (6) emery cloth; (7) tack cloth.

GREEN SANDPAPER Recently developed for use on latex paints and varnishes, green sandpaper won't gum up like other sandpapers do. It is available in fine to coarse grades.

TACK CLOTH A tack cloth looks like a slice of cheese in a plastic bag. Usually it comes with no instructions, one of the mystery materials sold at hardware and paint stores. Tack cloths are an absolute necessity for furniture painting and decorating. Composed of cheesecloth impregnated with a tacky substance, its purpose is to pick up all traces of dust. These cloths work so effectively, you may want them for dusting around the house.

Vacuum up any large quantities of dust. Then, remove the tack cloth from the package, but don't unfold. Instead, use the outside surfaces for wiping, until they are completely caked with dust. Then fold the tack cloth inside out and keep wiping. Continue wiping and refolding the cloth until it is completely used. Between uses, keep the cloth tightly packed in plastic so that it doesn't dry out.

You hate sanding, so why not just skip it? No one will know. Right?

Manual and Power Tools

TOOLS PLUS COMMON-SENSE PROTECTION EQUAL PROFESSIONAL RESULTS

MANUAL TOOLS If you are putting together a basic toolbox, the following tools are recommended. Start with a screwdriver, the type that stores several interchangeable bits in the handle. (Some of these have a ratcheting device that saves time, energy and wrist fatigue.) Next are the screws. Old furniture that has been repaired will often have mismatched screws, and no two pieces of new furniture seem to use the same type of screw. In a perfect world, there would be one type of screw, and it would be a Robertson – the square-slot type that stays on the screwdriver. A small hammer is handy for attaching wood trim and hammering in loose nails. Small- and medium-sized C-clamps, for clamping glued pieces, are a good toolbox staple. So are small and large paint scrapers for scraping loose finish, spreading adhesive and lifting stripped paint. A small, lightweight, fine-toothed hand saw is often needed for cutting various wood trims. A staple gun is also useful. Choose one that takes ⅜ in. (1 cm) staples. If you have a lot of stapling to do, consider a power stapler. (See Power Tools, below.) Acquire additional tools as you need them. Reduce frustration by storing tools in a toolbox that keeps them visible or has shallow drawers, as opposed

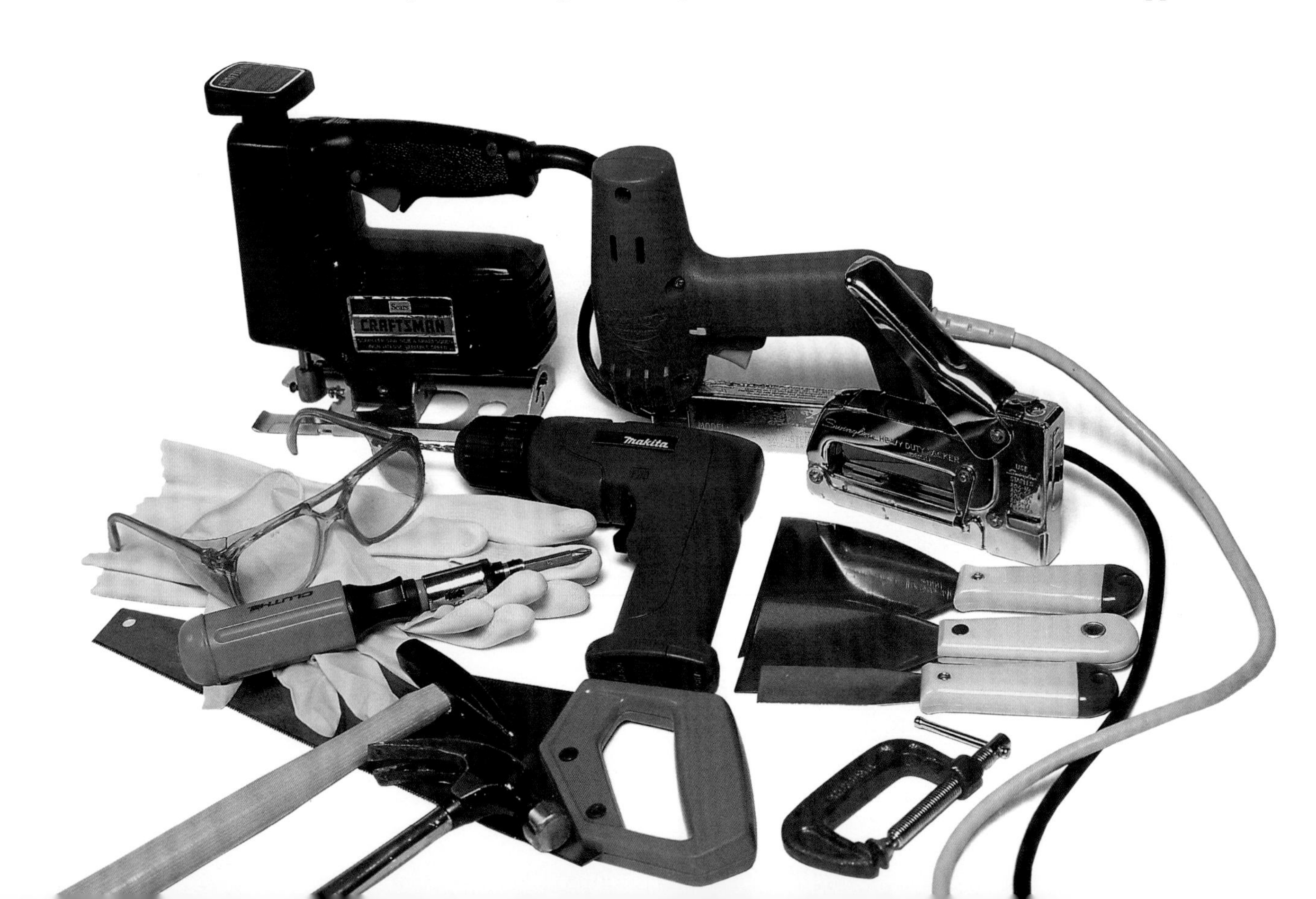

to the type with one deep box where tools become buried and difficult to find. There's a catch, however. For the toolbox to be effective, you have to put the tools back in when you're through.

POWER TOOLS

Very few power tools are required for furniture painting and refinishing. A small vibrating sander can be a handy substitute for manual sanding. Occasionally, a power drill will be required for drilling holes for hardware and leader-holes for screws. A cordless, lightweight drill with a keyless chuck is preferable. Purchase the appropriate drill bits for whatever you are drilling, wood or metal, and in the required size. A drill can also take the elbow grease out of screwing in screws. You'll need screwdriver drill bits to fit your drill. To cut plywood for tabletops or chair seats, use the appropriate saw: a table saw for straight cuts, and a jigsaw or scroll saw for curved cuts. No need to skip a project because you don't have a power saw. Many lumberyards will custom cut wood. If cutting metal, use a specialty blade. *When cutting with any type of saw, wear the necessary protective gear and watch those fingers.* If you have a big stapling job, such as a set of six chair cushions, consider springing for a power stapler.

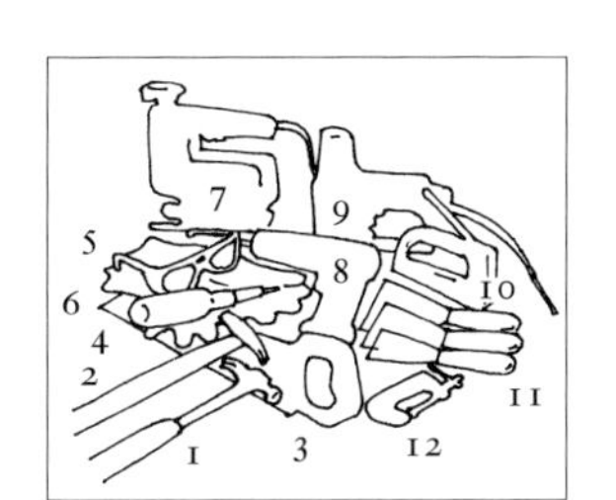

(1) 9 oz. hammer; (2) tacking hammer; (3) hand saw; (4) screwdriver; (5) safety goggles; (6) rubber gloves; (7) jigsaw (scroll saw); (8) power drill; (9) power stapler; (10) manual stapler; (11) paint scrapers; (12) C-clamp.

Unlike hand-held staplers, most power staplers take all staple sizes. The ease of operation makes the job breathtakingly fast.

PROTECTIVE GEAR

Always wear safety goggles when cutting metal, smashing tile for mosaic, or tackling any other task that can produce flying debris. When sanding, spray painting or using other materials that can produce airborne particles of paint or dust that could be inhaled, wear a paper mask that filters particles. To block both particles and fumes (or only fumes), wear a charcoal mask. For some jobs, like applying paint stripper or other toxic materials where the symbol of a hand turning into a skeleton appears on the label, gloves are an absolute necessity. Choose the heavy rubber kitchen-style gloves for these jobs. Gloves are not a necessity for most paint jobs, but many painters won't paint without them. Latex gloves – the ones that are disposable, stretchy, lightweight and thin – are perfect for painting. Wear these gloves for jobs that can irritate your hands, such as sanding, painting, rolling paint, or tiling. No more farmer's hands and wrecked manicures. If you develop a rash or hayfever-like symptoms, discontinue wearing latex gloves. You may have an allergy.

Buying tools needn't break the bank. Buy only what you need for each job, and consider renting one-job-only tools such as tile cutters or power saws.

Metallics

ANTIQUED AND PATINATED METALLICS ADD RADIANCE

METALLIC LEAF

The rich patina of gold leafing is no longer the exclusive domain of the highly trained sign painter or the refinishing specialist. Imitation gold and other metallic leaf, and the necessary components of adhesive and sealer, are available at art supply and craft stores. For genuine gold, try a framing supplier. Purchase compatible products all made by the same manufacturer. Incompatible products can cause chemical reactions that ruin the finish.

Applying metallic leaf is straightforward and simple, and the results are professional looking. The adhesive is applied to the surface area and allowed to cure for several minutes. It remains extremely tacky. The metallic leaf is laid over the adhesive and burnished to make contact with it. Excess leaf is brushed away with a small paint brush. Then the leaf is protected with a coat of sealer. Leafing is available in gold, silver, pewter and copper, all of which can be antiqued or left bright. To antique the leafing, purchase

antiquing paint or use watered-down artist's acrylics in a deep-brown shade on gold, or green on copper.

METALLIC PAINT

As an alternative to metallic leaf, paint-on metal (made from ground ore suspended in a liquid medium), available at art supply stores, provides a dense, convincing metallic finish. Don't confuse these paints with small jars of gold and silver hobby-type enamels. You'll know the right ones if they are displayed with the compatible patinas, sealer and etching fluid. Patinas include green or blue oxidation or rust. Choose instant iron, gold, copper or bronze. The labels on the jars of paint include instructions for using each product. A clear sealer, which acts as a primer, is brushed on first, followed by two coats of the metal. The metallic paint can be patinated in green or blue, or sealed as is. (See *Ivy League,* page 74, for copper.)

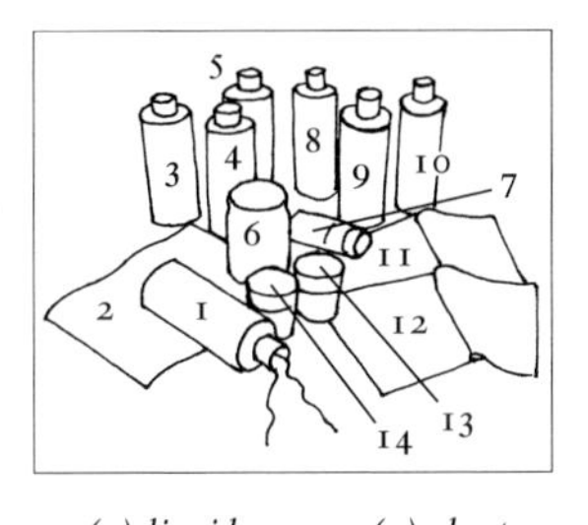

(1) liquid copper; (2) sheet copper; (3) patina blue; (4) primer-sealer; (5) etching fluid; (6) mica gel; (7) artist's acrylic paint; (8) liquid iron; (9) instant rust; (10) patina green; (11) copper leaf; (12) gold leaf; (13) sealer for leaf; (14) adhesive for leaf.

PATINA

Patina is the thin sheen on a copper or other surface, produced by age. Patinating metallic paint gives an aged and refined quality to a piece of furniture.

These treatments are usually applied to molded or carved-looking decorative pieces such as pedestals; however, they are also effective on flat surfaces. Blue and green patinas are available for copper metallic paint, and rust is available for iron. Purchase the patinas wherever you buy the metallic paint. All the patinas are very watery. When brushed onto the dry metallic paint, they begin their work, almost immediately oxidizing the metal. Apply sparingly, adding more coats to achieve the desired effect. Once the patina has finished the oxidizing process, usually three days, clear sealer is applied. Clear sealer can tone down the effect of the patina and kill the sheen of the metallic paint. It's a good idea first to do a test on cardboard to examine the effects of the sealer on the finish. If you don't seal the patinated metal, the treatment may transfer or be damaged by use.

SHEET COPPER

Try hobby shops as well as art supply and craft stores for finding sheet copper. This is the copper that hobbyists use for burnishing. The sheets are as thick as heavy paper and can be cut with heavy workshop or kitchen scissors. *When cutting this copper, be extremely careful.* The edges can be very sharp. Injuries are more painful and annoying than paper cuts. (Wearing a cast-off pair of leather gloves can help protect you.) The cut edges can be sanded dull with very fine sandpaper or an emery cloth. Sheet copper can be patinated with the same blue or green patina used on metallic paints. Before patinating the copper, treat it with an etching fluid, often called metal master, which is part of the metallic paint and patina family. Then follow the same steps for patinating metallic paint. (See *Art in Craft,* page 106, step 4.)

Metallics are most effective when used as an accent rather than as an all-over treatment.

Paint Products

Fast-Drying, Low-Odor, Easy-Clean-Up Paints, Additives and Varnishes Add To The Pleasure Of Painting

Latex Wall Paint Although the experts at the hardware store may insist you need oil-based paint, just keep in mind that they're probably not computer geniuses either. Times have changed. It is no longer necessary to endure the noxious fumes, glacial drying times and tedious clean-up of oil-based paints. The technology of water-based paint products means long-wearing paint in finishes from flat matte to high gloss; low odor; very fast drying and recoating times; and easy soap-and-water clean-up.

Whether you purchase a can of acrylic paint (plastic emulsion) or latex paint (synthetic rubber emulsion) at the paint store – both types are popularly referred to as latex – expect to apply two coats for solid coverage. Don't be alarmed that the paint is a light color in the can. It will dry darker. Choose a low-luster to glossy finish for furniture. Avoid flat finishes, which show fingerprints and scuff marks. Any water-based paint should be well stirred or shaken before using. Latex paint dries quickly to the touch – usually an hour – but it should be allowed to dry several hours before recoating. Consult the label for precise drying times. Water-based paints remain vulnerable and need to cure for at least thirty days before being washed or subjected to wear and tear.

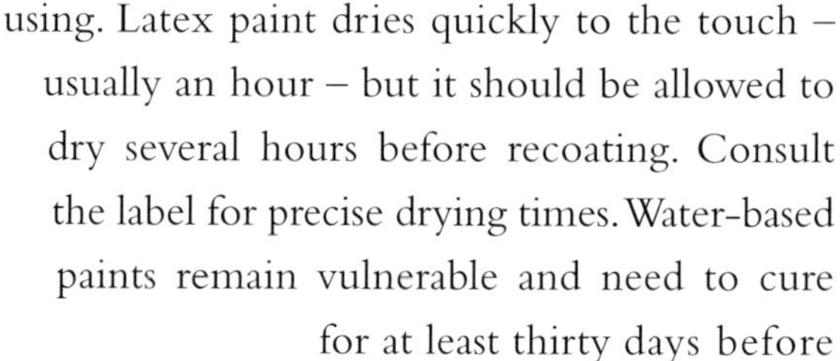

Acrylic Wall Paint This paint can be bought by the can at paint stores. Because it is water based, it is generally (but improperly) referred to as latex. Check the label for the actual contents. More expensive than latex paint, pure acrylic wall paint is considered the highest quality of most paint lines. But the reality is that when it dries, it has a rubbery finish that tends to stick to objects that come in contact with the surface for any length of time, lifting the paint (a problem on furniture). A better bet is a combination of acrylic and latex. You'll get the best qualities of both types of paint. Like latex paint, acrylic needs to cure for thirty days.

Artist's Acrylics Originally intended as an alternative to artist's oils, acrylic paint has developed as a versatile medium in its own right. Available in a huge range of premixed colors and incredibly fast drying, their compatibility with latex paint makes artist's acrylics ideal for creative furniture treatments. Artist's acrylics can be used straight from the tube for an oil-paint texture or thinned with water for watercolor washes and glazes. They can also be used for stenciling, block printing, freehand painting or texturing. Generally sold in small pots and tubes, these acrylics offset the need to buy a large can of latex paint, which is too much paint for detail work.

(1) artist's acrylics in tubes; (2) artist's acrylics in pots; (3) colored glazes; (4) latex paint; (5) glaze; (6) extender; (7) shellac; (8) spray paint; (9) primer; (10) acrylic mediums; (11) varnish; (12) gel.

Melamine Paint The popularity of plastic laminate, particleboard furniture and countertops has helped create a generation of new high-adhesion paints, referred to as melamine paints. Unlike most other paints, which lose their grip and peel, these cling tenaciously to plastic surfaces. Always degloss the melamine surface by sanding with fine sandpaper (220 grade or finer) before applying the paint. Melamine paints vary from store to store. If a label indicates that a primer is necessary, use an ultra-high-adhesion, white-pigmented, shellac-based primer for best results. Allow melamine paint to cure for two to four weeks before subjecting to wear and tear or washing. If melamine paint is not available, latex paint can be substituted – so long as the melamine surface has been deglossed by sanding and a coat of ultra-high-adhesion, white-pigmented, shellac-based primer is applied first.

The durable quality of artist's acrylics, their availability in small quantities, and their compatibility with other paints make them perfect for furniture treatments.

Spray Paint Spray paints are ideal for painting pieces of furniture with spindles or intricate molding. Spray painting imparts a dense, smooth, even coat in a range of finishes from low luster to high gloss. It also eliminates the drips, gaps and sags usually associated with brush painting.

While graffiti may have given spray painting a bad name, this art form created a demand for spray paint that has benefited the furniture refinisher with a wealth of low-odor, low-toxicity acrylic spray products in a huge range of colors. Purchase spray paint at hardware, art supply and craft stores. Also available in spray form are textured treatments such as granite and marble; paints for covering metal or rust; varnishes; and fast-drying, crystal clear lacquers. (See *Spray Painting,* page 44, for more information on the application of spray paint.) For the avid spray painter, special nozzles giving narrow to wide coverage are available at art stores that cater to the graffiti trade.

Paint Removers

NOT LIKE THE OLD DAYS – GENTLE STRIPPING AGENTS AND EFFECTIVE TOOLS MAKE PAINT REMOVAL FUN (ALMOST)

PAINT STRIPPERS

If the idea of paint strippers conjures up visions of vats of steaming toxic waste, it's been a while since you tried stripping paint. There are strippers that smell like citrus fruit, and some are non-toxic enough that wearing gloves is optional. Welcome as these advancements are, stripping furniture is still a messy job, especially if the piece has intricate detail or many layers of paint and varnish. A piece of furniture with either historic or design integrity is, however, worth the journey into slime. Stripping a good basic piece buried under several coats of badly applied paint is also worthwhile, because it cannot be repainted until the many layers are removed. But you can also partially strip such a piece, allowing sections of layered color to show through. This treatment is not only interesting and attractive, but it reveals the history of the piece. An example of this technique is shown on page 106.

The old way of stripping was called dip and strip. The whole piece was placed in a trough of heavy-duty toxic chemical stripper. This procedure often unglued joints and had caustic effects on the underlying wood. Most strippers today are much more gentle. Choose a gel stripper, which will cling to vertical surfaces. Placing plastic wrap over the stripper can speed the curing time. Just check first that the stripper doesn't eat the plastic.

PROTECTIVE GEAR Paint stripper will destroy the finish on your floor. Do the job over several layers of paper (newspaper is fine), with a layer of plastic or, even better (since some strippers dissolve plastic), an old bedsheet on top. Decant the stripper to paint it on. Pour it into crockery, not plastic. Wear heavy rubber gloves for this job, the kitchen type. Avoid latex surgical gloves unless you are certain the stripper won't eat through them. Safety goggles are also recommended. When you brush the stripper on and scrape off loosened paint, some particles can become airborne.

(1) stripping brush; (2) rubber gloves; (3) organic stripper; (4) gel stripper; (5) safety goggles; (6) paint scrapers.

TOOLS Using the proper tools will make the stripping go much faster and easier. In the first stages of the stripping, a medium-sized paint scraper is needed for lifting the bubbled, loose paint. Next, a hard plastic stripping sponge, which resembles a block of petrified spaghetti, is ideal to use along with the stripper to help lift paint. When most of the paint has been removed, use a stripping brush along with the stripping sponge. This brush resembles a barbecue-grill cleaner, with brass bristles (they won't rust) on one side and nylon bristles on the other. The nylon brush side is ideal for giving the piece a thorough rubdown. The brass bristles remove the last particles of paint and varnish from any carving and trim, and from the grain of the wood. When using scrapers and other sharp tools, remember to let the stripper do the work. Overly enthusiastic scraping can damage fine or soft wood, defeating the purpose of stripping, which is to reveal the natural, unspoiled beauty of the wood.

Hold it! Don't strip that antique! However worn and beaten-up the furniture may be, original paint on an antique adds greatly to its authenticity and value.

Specialty Products

From the Inspired to the Bizarre, New Products Are Created to Fulfill the Painter's Every Need

Kits A tremendous number of kits are available for techniques such as crackle, block printing, marbling, sponging and stenciling. Many of these kits are adequate for the painter, particularly if only a small area is to be painted, eliminating the need to buy large quantities of products that will go unused. However, some of the kits are pricey and don't live up to their promises, with poor instructions and materials that just don't work. Many of these techniques are actually quite simple to perform, require readily available ingredients and are demonstrated in this book.

Special Applicators Manufacturers are scrambling to keep pace with the demand for innovative paint applicators. Aside from the usual brushes and rollers, there are combs (for creating striping and basketweave effects) and raised wood-grain patterns to be rolled and dragged. Most unusual are rollers that have plastic floral shapes riveted to them, reminiscent of a 1960s-era bathing cap. These rollers are used to create texture by layering similar paint colors, thinned with glaze, with the plastic attachments producing a subtle, semiregular pattern. Various sponges, rags and texturing brushes are available too, as are foam applicators for painting edges, corners and flat areas.

SPECIALTY PAINT Fashion designers like Ralph Lauren and Laura Ashley, who have become lifestyle/interior designers, have come out with signature lines of top-quality water-based paints in painter-inspiring rich colors. These paints are created to complement the housewares that the designers also produce. Although this approach to choosing a paint color may seem excessive to some, others find it reassuring and exciting, trusting that the results will be exactly as expected and that the decor and paint will be tasteful and will harmonize perfectly. Other paint manufacturers are producing innovative paints with unlimited possibilities for application. There are very thick iridescent paints, which are applied in layers with a trowel, sanded and glazed to a glasslike sheen. There are paints with tiny flecks of suspended color, which are made to be layered with similarly toned glazes to produce wonderful depth and suspended texture. There are also a variety of spray-paint effects, including a granitelike composition that comes in kit form. There is even spray-on marble veining, although it looks rather like a mix of hair and mushy spaghetti. Instead of trying to create marble veins with it, the creative painter could have fun with the effect in other unusual ways.

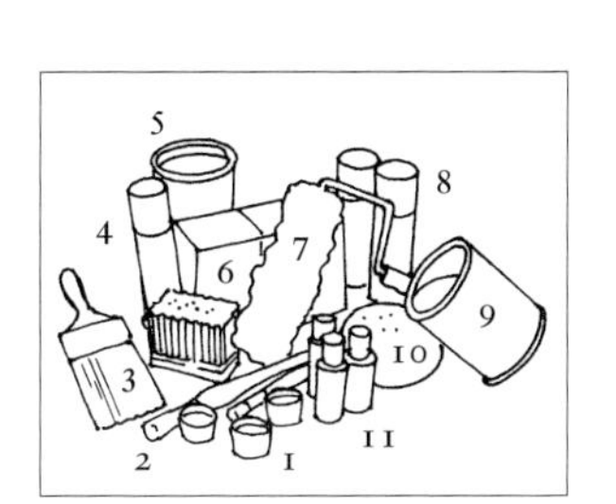

(1) stencil cream paints; (2) stencil brush; (3) texturing brushes; (4) marbling spray; (5) flecked paint; (6) marbling kit; (7) texturing roller; (8) spray granite; (9) texturing paint; (10) synthetic sponge; (11) colored glazes.

STENCILING MATERIALS Purchase a precut stencil from the huge selection available, or design and cut your own. To cut your own stencils, buy stencil plastic at an art supply or craft store – the lightweight, flexible blue plastic that is semitransparent for tracing designs – and use an X-acto or a utility knife or small, pointed scissors. Lightweight cardboard can be substituted for the plastic. To execute the stencil, use any type of paint you wish: spray paint for smooth even coverage, acrylic or latex paint applied with an artist's paint brush for a freehand look with brushstrokes, or stencil cream paint applied with a stencil (stipple) brush for dense smooth coverage. The spray and acrylic paints dry quickly, while the cream paint can take as long as a week to dry. Use spray glue to provide a tacky backing on the stencil. (See *Pretty Fantastic,* page 86.)

Don't be intimidated by the multitude of new products at the paint store. Many can add substantially to your creative pursuits.

Painting Basics

Most projects in this book will refer you to this section to prepare, prime and, in some cases, paint your furniture with a base coat of paint. This base coat is the groundwork for your decorative treatment.

Step one is the preparation. Virtually every piece of furniture needs some preparation before your finish is applied, whether you're repairing wobbly parts, removing doors, hinges and hardware, deglossing a shiny surface, or sanding raw wood.

Step two is applying the primer. Most furniture – varnished or painted wooden pieces, melamine pieces, or unpainted wooden furniture – requires priming. Exceptions include furniture with a stable finish that will be fully covered in fabric or paper, unpainted wooden furniture that will be stained, and furniture to be painted and then antiqued by sanding. Each project will tell you when to prime; then you can refer to this section for more information.

Step three is the painting. Paint is applied (usually two coats) over the primer in the same manner as the primer was applied. After the base coat of paint has been applied, the creative and inventive stage of adding decorative effects and treatments begins.

Skipping the preparation stage now may haunt you later.

Preparation

In the final analysis, the preparation of the furniture – fixing loose parts and preparing the surface for painting – is more important than any painting or decorating. Avoid the temptation to skip the prep stage of painting. It will yield consequences (that mom warned you about) of the same variety as building a house on sand, eating dessert before the main course, or sleeping in an unmade bed. Different varieties of furniture will require different types of preparation. Read through this section to determine how much and which types of preparation your particular piece of furniture needs. Although many painters dread this part of the job, once it is out of the way, the paint and decorative treatments can be done with a clear conscience.

Purchase new hardware if desired. If the piece has wooden knobs, consider painting them.

Right at the start, set up a comfortable, well-lit work area. Keep the work space as flexible as possible, with moveable light sources and a convenient table on which to work. You may wish to call off the bridge game and abscond with the card table. It's ideal for putting all but enormous items of furniture at a comfortable working height. Its small scale makes furniture accessible from all sides, and it can be folded up and tucked away when not needed. Keep a supply of dropsheets handy. Old large, non-slip bedsheets are good. Plastic or paper can be used, but don't use newspaper. The printer's ink will transfer to your paint job.

MATERIALS

The following tools and materials may be required.

- screwdriver
- machine oil
- new hardware and screws
- wood filler
- small paint scraper (or putty knife), wide paint scraper
- fine sandpaper (220 grade)
- sanding block
- wooden matchsticks
- white carpenter's glue
- clamps or a bungy cord
- power drill
- deglossing compound (TSP or other liquid sandpaper), rubber gloves
- tack cloth

1 *Drawers*

Remove drawers, marking their position (top, center, bottom, etc.) on the back panel. As a result of wear and tear or how they were built, drawers will often fit properly only in their original slots.

2 *Hardware*

Unscrew and remove all hardware. This includes removing doors by unscrewing hinges. On a dropleaf table, remove the hinges and the contraptions that keep the leaves up. Hinges should be cleaned and oiled. If a tabletop is removable, the painting will be easier if the top is removed and painted separately from the base.

3 *Filler*

If holes left by old hardware don't correspond to the new hardware, use wood filler and a small paint scraper or putty knife to fill the holes. Also fill any gouges in the surface of the piece. Sand the wood filler smooth and level with the surface, using fine sandpaper.

Fill the screw holes of loose door hinges with the wooden ends of matchsticks and carpenter's glue. Allow to dry before replacing the hinges. Hinges can also be shifted when they are replaced.

4 *Fixing loose parts*

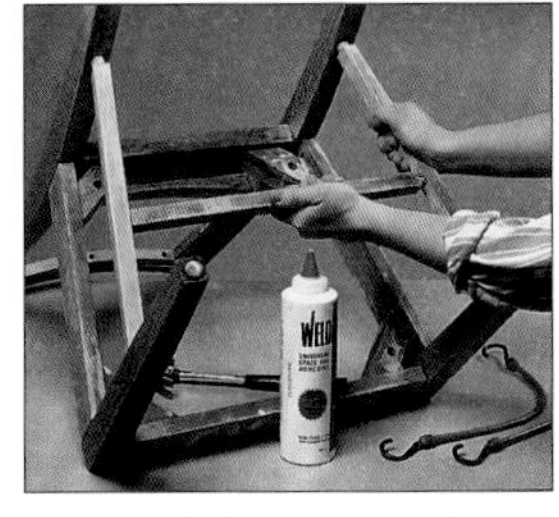

Loose desktops and dresser tops are caused by lifting the furniture by the top instead of the base. Reattach a loose dresser top by replacing the existing screws with fatter, not longer, ones. Reglue loose joins in a chair by levering the join apart, cleaning it as much as possible, then applying carpenter's glue to the join and clamping it shut. (If you don't own clamps, you can wrap tightly with a bungy cord.) Glue and clamp loose trim. Allow all glue to dry overnight.

Loose, wobbly table legs are caused by dragging the table instead of lifting it. There are many different constructions for table legs. Try to figure out how the table and legs are constructed. Glue and clamp all joins and tighten or replace all screws.

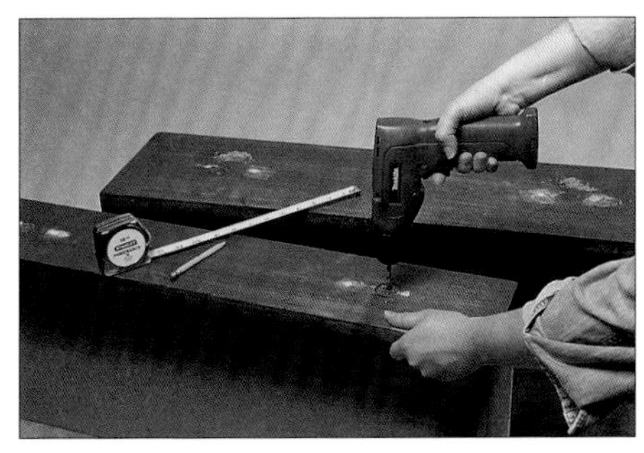

Measure and drill holes for new hardware, if needed.

5 *Preparing the finish*

Granny furniture – old, dark wood – should be given the fingernail test. Scratch the varnish with your fingernail. It should not be marked or lifted. If it is, this loose, crumbly finish will flake when painted, taking the paint with it. Scrape off the loose varnish with a wide paint scraper – a fast job. Then sand the surface smooth with fine sandpaper, either by hand or with a sanding block.

If the furniture has a high-gloss or plastic laminate finish, it will require light sanding to allow better adhesion between the paint and the furniture surface. Sand with fine sandpaper, in the direction of the grain on bare wood (sanding across the grain can create deep scratches), and lengthwise on painted pieces.

If you really hate the dust and the effort of sanding and your furniture has a medium- to low-luster finish, clean and degloss your furniture with a deglossing compound such as TSP. Mix the granules according to instructions on the label. Wearing rubber gloves, wash down all glossy areas, rinsing well with clean water. Allow the furniture to dry overnight.

Vacuum and clean the whole piece of furniture, both inside and out. Remove all remaining dust by wiping the piece with a tack cloth. If desired, wash the piece with a damp cloth and a gentle cleaner. Allow to dry overnight.

Cats seem to gravitate to the laps of those who want them least. Naturally, they're also drawn to fresh paint. Put puss out.

Priming and Painting

Applying a coat of primer before painting is a necessary step for most projects. Exceptions include furniture to be antiqued by sanding away paint to reveal bare wood, and unpainted wooden furniture to be stained. Primer adheres more tenaciously to the furniture's surface than paint does, to provide a strong bond and an even skin. The paint can then flow onto the primer without patchiness or an uneven texture.

Primer and paint should be applied by the same method. For instance, if the furniture is simple with flat surfaces, both primer and paint should be applied with brush and roller. If the furniture has intricate carving, trim, or spindles, spray primer and spray paint should be used. Don't be discouraged by the streaky, uneven quality of primer when you put it on. Apply primer swiftly and avoid the temptation to redo areas. Primer sets and dries quickly, and reworking will tear up the surface. Once the primer is dry, the furniture can be given one or two coats of water-based paint as a base coat. If your furniture has a plastic laminate finish, use melamine paint for the base coat. (See *Melamine Paint,* page 27.) Before adding other treatments, allow the coats of paint to dry for the time specified by the manufacturer.

Touching wet paint is a universal temptation, so devise strategies to keep yourself away while items are drying. Paint just before bedtime, for example. And remember, mistakes are the mother of inventive solutions.

MATERIALS

The following tools and materials may be required.

- small quantity of white shellac
- easy-release painter's tape or masking tape
- quart (litre) high-adhesion, water-based primer; or spray primer; or, for plastic laminate surfaces, if primer is suggested on the label, white-pigmented, shellac-based primer
- painting tools:
  - -paint brush, 1½ in. (4 cm) wide, for water-based paint
  - -roller handle, 4 in. (10 cm) wide, and short-pile sleeves
  - -roller tray to fit roller
- quart (litre) eggshell or satin finish latex paint in the color of your choice
- quart (litre) non-yellowing, water-based varnish
- paste wax, buffing cloth

1 *Choosing the primer*

If your piece has molding, spindles or carved detail, you may wish to use spray primer. (Follow the instructions for *Spray Painting*, page 44.)

2 *Priming removable pieces*

Seal any knots on raw wood with shellac before priming.

Stir primer thoroughly before applying it. Primer should be applied to all areas that will be painted.

Start with removable pieces, such as doors or drawers. Lay doors or other flat sections on supports and mask off any sections that are to remain unpainted.

If the drawers are clean, prime only the fronts and their edges. If the drawer interiors are grungy, paint them with primer.

Use the paint brush to cut-in with primer, painting all inside joins and corners that aren't accessible to a roller. (See *Brush Painting*, page 40.) Then use a roller to prime the flat areas up to the brushwork. (See *Roller Painting*, page 42.)

The exterior sides can be primed if desired, but make sure there is enough space between chest and drawer. (Adding coats of primer and paint to the sides can cause drawers to bind.) Water-based primers and paints dry quickly. Wash brushes when they're not in use.

3 *Priming the body*

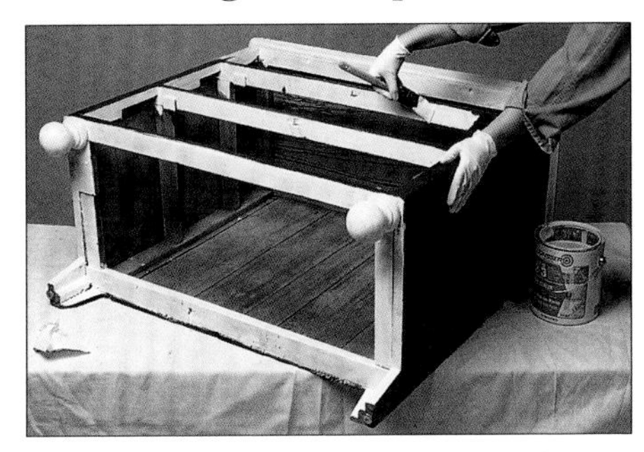

Bottoms up. Whatever the type of furniture, from chairs to hutches to tables, start priming the body of the piece of furniture from the bottom. Lay chests and cabinets on their backs and turn chairs and tables upside-down. (If the furniture is heavy, get some help lifting it.) Using a brush, cut-in all corners and places that are inaccessible with a roller. Then roller paint the primer up to the brushwork on all surfaces that you can comfortably reach. Priming the backs and interiors of cabinets, desks and dressers is optional.

Stand the piece upright. Cut-in and roller paint all remaining surfaces. Wash all paint utensils with soap and warm water. Allow the primer to dry.

4 *Painting*

Repeat steps 1 and 2, now using latex paint. Allow to dry and apply a second coat if necessary.

5 *Varnishing and finishing*

Continue, painting and decorating your piece of furniture, or if the piece is to be left a solid color, protect the paint and enrich the color by applying a non-yellowing, water-based varnish. (See *Varnishing*, page 48.)

Attach the hardware.

Binding may occur where paint comes into contact with other paint. In such areas, apply one or two heavy coats of paste wax and buff.

Paint the hardest-to-get-at areas first. There'll be less paint on the painter and more on the furniture.

Brush Painting

In spite of the numerous advances in paint tools and products, the most necessary and versatile tool is still the paint brush. But don't get caught up in brushmania. It's not necessary to buy an arsenal of expensive brushes for painting furniture. Use a medium-width brush with an angled cut to the bristles for cutting-in and for painting flat sections; an artist's square-tipped brush for narrow areas and detail work; and a fine-point artist's brush for freehand, intricate painting. While full-coverage painting is usually executed with a combination of brush and roller, sometimes brush painting is necessary to produce brushstrokes, desirable in many antiquing and rustic treatments. (See *Painting Tools,* page 24; *Specialty Products,* page 32.)

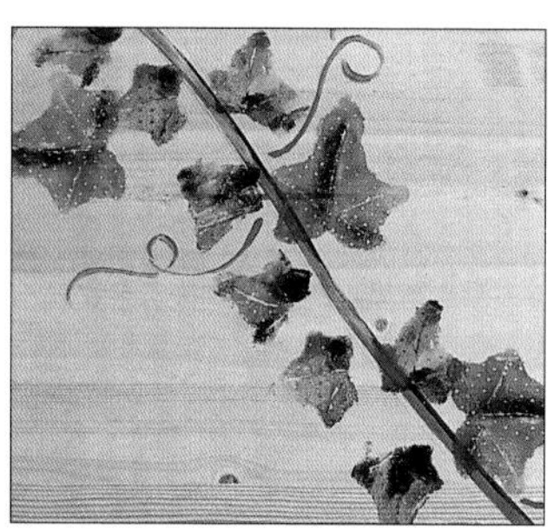

Creating with a brush adds individuality and personality to an otherwise predictable paint treatment.

There is no foolproof way to achieve a perfect paint job with a brush. There are, however, approaches to brush painting that will garner a smoother, more even coat with fewer drips and sags. Purchasing good-quality brushes, made to be used with your type of paint, either oil- or water-based, is a good start.

MATERIALS

The following tools and materials may be required.

- quart (litre) eggshell or satin finish latex paint in the color of your choice
- paint brush, 1½ in. (4 cm) wide, for water-based paint
- tube of acrylic paint in the color of your choice
- artist's brushes, medium square-tipped or fine point
- chalk or colored pencil

1 *Brush painting a flat area*

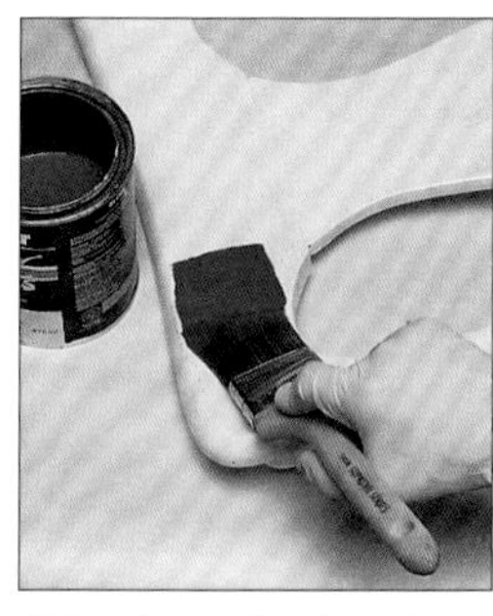

Stir the latex paint. Dip the paint brush into the paint to a level of about one-third to one-half of the bristles. Drag one side of the bristles against the lip of the can when removing the brush from the can.

Lay the wet side of the brush on an open part of the furniture, inside an edge. Brush the paint outward, brushing the length of the area, not the width.

Brush toward and over edges, if possible. If the brush is dragged against an edge, as shown in the photo, the paint will form drips.

Continue brushing, quickly and deftly smoothing the paint. Reload the brush as needed. Keep a constant watch for drips, swiping them away with the brush. Water-based paint sets quickly. Avoid brushing over the same area several times. Overbrushing will create deep brush-strokes in the setting paint. Finish painting one section of the piece at a time.

2 *Cutting-in*

When painting joins and corner detail, load a small amount of paint onto the brush and use the longer point of the brush's angled tip to coax paint into the corner, dragging the brush alongside the join. The angled cut on the brush suits this technique, especially when cutting-in on the insides of drawers and other pieces with many angles and inside corners. Watch for drips and sags, swiping them away with the brush.

3 *Painting details*

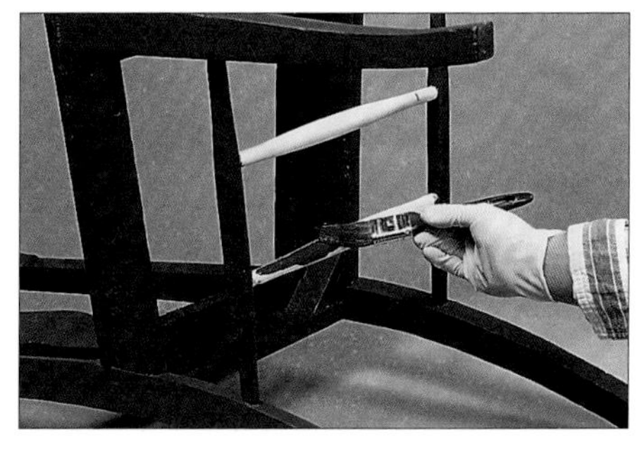

Though spray paint is usually best for spindles and other ornamental work, sometimes details must match the overall effect of a brush-painted piece. Load the brush with a small amount of paint. Holding the brush on an angle, drag it in a downward motion along the spindle, depositing the paint in a long bead.

Quickly brush out the paint to an even coat. Watch for any drips and sags, brushing them out.

4 *Freehand brushwork*

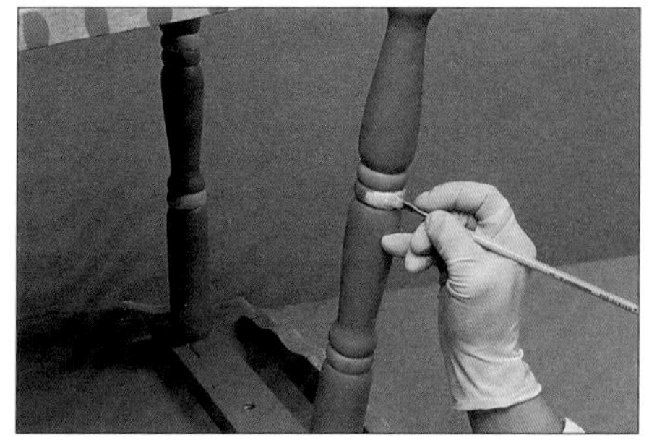

Freehand painting in contrasting colors is attractive on carved or turned details. Position at eye level the area to be painted. Use an artist's brush of a size suitable for the area, and artist's acrylics or latex paint. Thin the paint if needed so that it flows easily from the brush, but is not watery. Try to maintain a steady hand. Keep edges even and end the color at a natural break.

To paint freehand designs, such as dots or trailing vines, draw your design first with a piece of chalk or a colored pencil. Use a fine-point artist's brush and acrylic or latex paint, thinned if necessary to flow from the brush. Dip the point of the brush into the paint. With your hand raised (laying the heel of your hand on the table creates cramped shapes), apply pressure on the brush to obtain the thickness of the line desired. Paint the line, using the chalk line as a guide only. Following the chalk line too closely will cause hesitation, resulting in tentative lines.

Rollers are available in a wide variety of sizes. Choose one that fits the job.

Roller Painting

The roller is undoubtedly one of the most important painting tools, second only to the paint brush. It provides fast, even coverage and smooth texture without brushstrokes. A relatively recent invention, the roller has revolutionized painting. But until recently, roller painting was viewed only as a fast way to cover large areas. New, creative ways of using this versatile tool are now being explored to produce repetitive patterns and textured layering of color. For painting furniture, purchase a small roller handle with removable short-pile sleeves to fit. Buy two or more sleeves, because most are good for only one application of paint. Choose a paint tray to fit the roller. A paint tray is better than a paper plate or other disposable substitutes, because its reservoir and textured ramp provide more even distribution and better control of the paint. First, with a brush, cut-in on far corners and other hard-to-get-at places. Then use the roller to apply primer or paint, but not varnish. Varnish should always be brushed on.

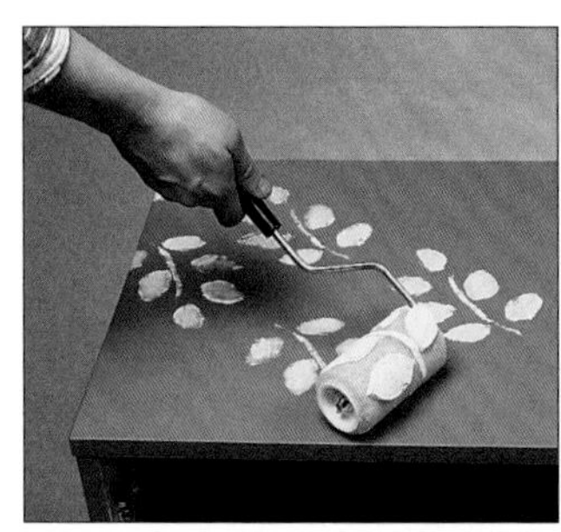

The smooth texture of a roller-painted surface provides an excellent base for creative treatments such as roller block printing.

MATERIALS

The following tools and materials may be required.

- quart (litre) eggshell or satin finish latex paint in the color of your choice
- roller handle, 4 in. (10 cm) wide, and short-pile sleeves to fit
- roller tray to fit roller
- fine sandpaper (220 grade or finer), tack cloth

1 *Ready to roll*

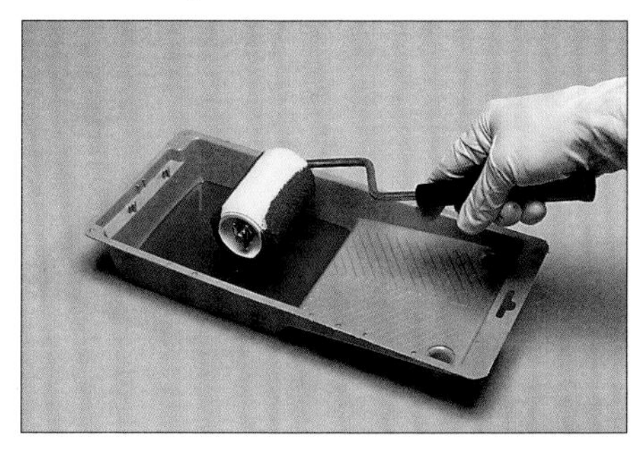

To prevent air bubbles from forming in the paint and to remove any loose roller-sleeve lint, dampen the sleeve and rub it as dry as possible with a paper towel.

Pour paint into the reservoir of the tray, filling it about half full. Dip the roller sleeve into the tray and roll it so that the full sleeve is coated in paint.

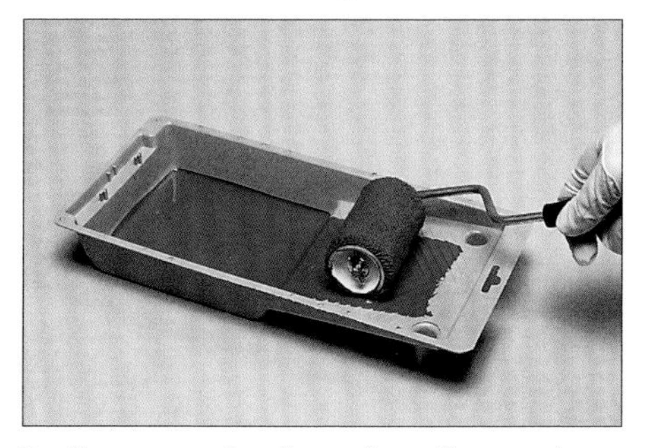

Roll excess paint from the roller on the ramp of the tray, but don't overdo it. The roller should still hold a good quantity of paint.

2 *Applying an even coat*

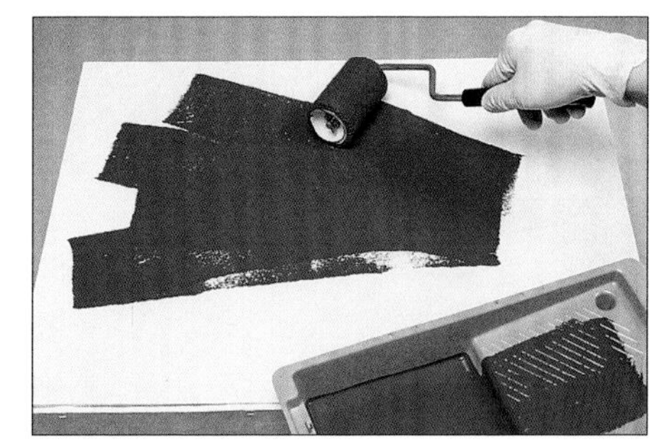

Position the roller on a surface of the furniture, inside the edges. Beginning at this central point, roll the paint outward in a triangular fashion, criss-crossing previous lines. This technique will give even texture and prevent a grid from appearing. Don't try to achieve full coverage in only one coat. Excessive paint that isn't rolled out will create stretch marks – an undesirable texture.

Apply moderate, even pressure. Let the roller do the work. It is better to reload the roller with paint than to squeeze more paint from it. Heavy pressure will create railroad tracks – a double line of heavy paint formed along the sides of the roller.

3 *Roller logic*

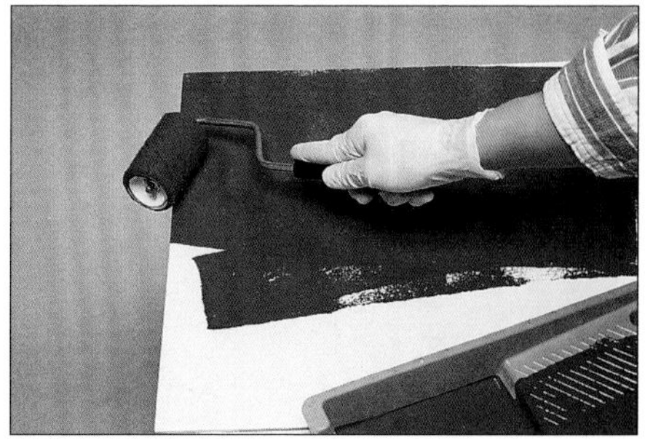

Roll toward and over edges, instead of pulling the roller against an edge. Rolling against an edge creates drips. As you roll, be on the lookout for drips and either swipe them with a brush or roll them out.

Continue rolling, overlapping each new roller of paint over the edge of the last, until the full surface is covered. Avoid the temptation to reroll a wet section. Water-based paint sets quickly, and rerolling will tear up the surface. Instead, allow to dry and apply another coat. For an ultrasmooth finish, lightly sand the first coat with fine sandpaper when it is completely dry and wipe clean with a tack cloth before applying the second coat. Between coats, keep paint wet by placing the tray and roller in a plastic bag, squishing the bag to eliminate air.

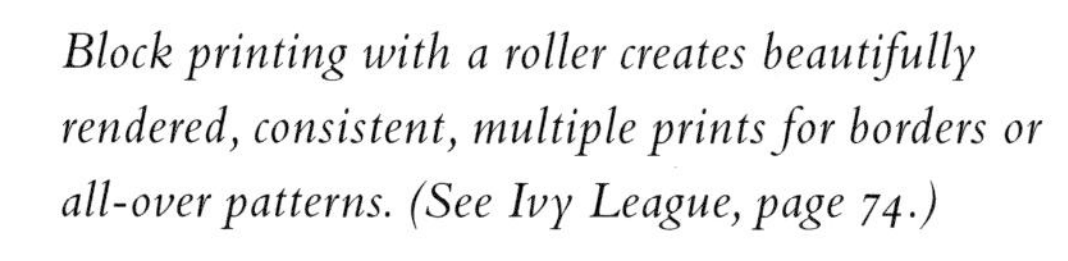

Block printing with a roller creates beautifully rendered, consistent, multiple prints for borders or all-over patterns. (See Ivy League, page 74.)

Be sure to check the direction of the nozzle.

Spray Painting

Spray painting gives smooth, dense coverage to furniture with ornamental carving and texture. The invasive nature of spray paint allows it to go where a brush can't reach, quickly and without drips or sags from brushing. Wherever you spray paint, large dropsheets are required to avoid home-and-garden decorating by default. Only a small portion of the paint coming from the nozzle connects with your furniture. The overspray really travels, settling on surfaces and in tiny crevices. So tape dropsheets together and cover everything that might catch drifting paint. Also make sure you work in a well-ventilated environment to avoid asphyxiating the canary. Spray painting outside is fine, unless it is too breezy. A garage with an open door is best. Indoors, several open windows, or an open window with a fan, will help. Inevitably, a certain amount of fumes and spray will be inhaled, simply because of the painter's proximity to the spray can. A paper mask will screen out spray paint particles, while a charcoal mask will filter out both paint and the fumes of the paint.

The smooth lacquerlike quality of spray paint is perfect for a background of lattice. *See page 96.*

Most sprays don't require primer. But if your furniture has a patchy, uneven finish, spray with primer first. Acrylic-based sprays, available in both low-luster and glossy finishes, are superb for most furniture. Choose a specialty spray paint to cover rust or to add texture. If the local paint store has a limited selection of finishes or types of spray paint, try hardware outlets or art supply or craft stores.

MATERIALS

The following tools and materials may be required.

- dropsheets
- charcoal mask or painter's mask
- one or more cans of acrylic spray paint
- one or more cans of spray primer
- one or more cans of rust-covering spray paint
- steel-wool pad

1 *Getting started*

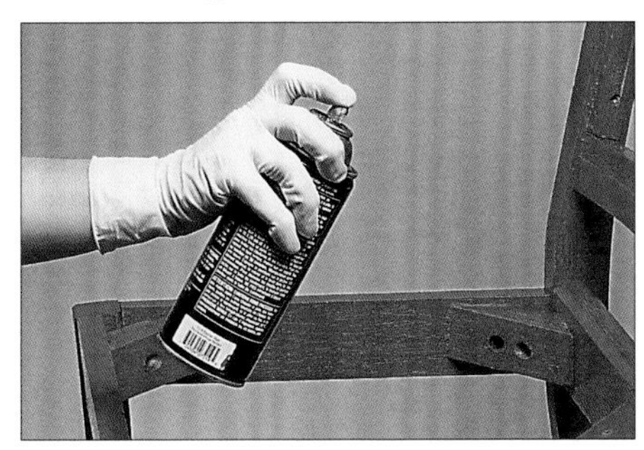

Attention allergy sufferers: a charcoal mask to eliminate fumes is recommended. If the label indicates flammable (inflammable) or explosive, do not work where there may be open flame, including a flame as tiny as the pilot light on a stove, furnace or water heater.

Using plastic dropsheets, old bedsheets or paper (not newspaper because the ink will transfer to the painted piece), cover every surface around your furniture piece that may catch some stray spray or overspray.

Shake the can for at least two full minutes. Test by spraying paint on a piece of paper. The first few sprays may appear watery until the paint makes its way up the tube.

2 *Spray primer*

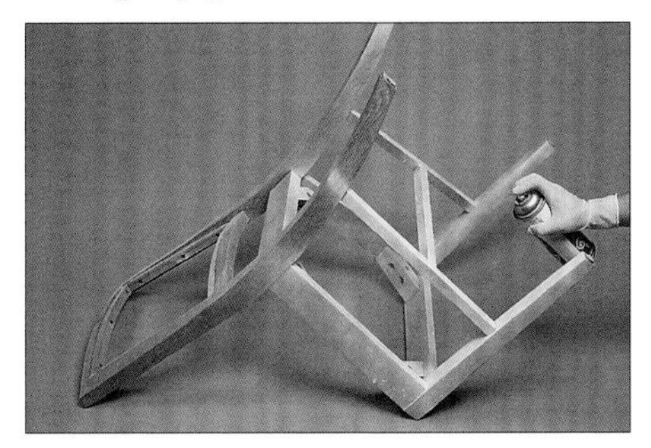

If you use a primer, apply one coat. Primer dries very fast. You should be able to turn the piece of furniture as you work, spraying all surfaces quickly. Allow to dry thoroughly.

3 *Rust-covering spray paint*

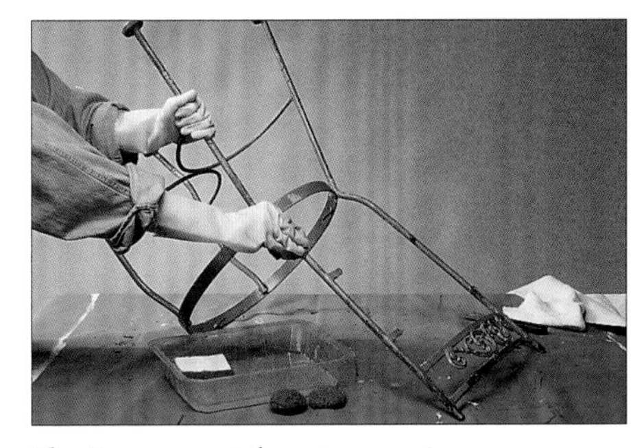

If using a special rust-covering spray paint, remove as much rust as possible from the furniture with water and a steel-wool pad. Rinse well and allow to dry. Follow the directions on the label for application and drying times.

4 *Spray painting, phase 1*

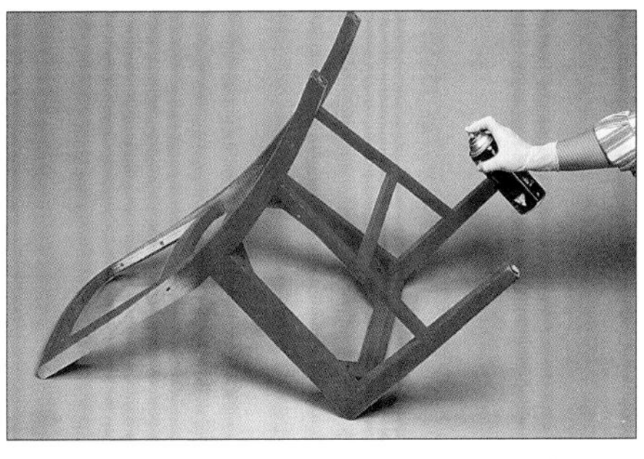

Position the piece of furniture upside-down on the dropsheet. (If the furniture is heavy, get some help lifting it.) Holding the can about 10 in. (25 cm) away from the object, depress the nozzle fully, spraying the furniture with a light, even coat. Spraying too heavily will create drips and sags. Several light coats are better than one heavy one. Spray all visible surfaces without moving the piece.

Recoat while the piece is in the same position. Check the label. The recoating instructions on most spray paints say to apply another coat within one hour. If you miss that deadline, you must wait three days to recoat. Apply as many coats as required for dense, even coverage.

5 *Spray painting, phase 2*

Allow the paint to become dry to the touch. Turn the piece of furniture upright and repeat step 4. Continue until all surfaces are covered. Allow to dry thoroughly.

The most beautiful stains can come from unexpected sources.

Staining Wood

The opaque density of paint invites creativity, but don't overlook the effect of stain on bare wood. Simple and very fast to apply, stains appear dark in their liquid form, yet are transparent when they dry. But transparent doesn't mean invisible. Stain not only provides color. As it is absorbed into the wood, it also accentuates the grain and markings. What was a bland, bare piece of pine five minutes ago is now a fascinating and intricate natural work of art. Most commercial stains for wood are natural brown wood shades. However, dramatic jewel tones, rustic colors or rich shades can be had from berries or fabric dyes.

Paint treatments such as block printing add color and an extra dimension to stained wood. *(See Ivy League, page 74)*

After applying a commercial stain, protect the surface with wax, oil or varnish. Many stains are available already mixed with varnish or oil – making staining and finishing a one-step process. Ask at your paint store about these mixes. Always varnish natural or bright-colored stains to protect the finish and prevent transfer of color.

MATERIALS

The following tools and materials may be required.

- commercial stain in an appropriate quantity
- fine sandpaper (180 to 220 grade)
- sanding block
- tack cloth
- small quantity of white shellac or other sealer
- wooden stir stick
- paint brush
- rags
- quart (litre) non-yellowing, water-based varnish;or furniture oil or wax and buffing cloth

I *Getting started*

Start with completely bare wood, free of paint, varnish or glue. If the wood was previously painted and stripped it must be free of all paint residue, and the surface should be lightly sanded to open the grain. Unpainted wooden furniture is often sealed – the result of saws used to cut the wood – giving the wood a slightly shiny surface. Wood that is sealed will absorb stain unevenly, giving the surface a patchy appearance. Sand unpainted furniture lightly with fine sandpaper to open the grain.

Holding the sandpaper flat in your hand or using a sanding block, sand the surface lightly with fine sandpaper in the direction of the grain. (Sanding across the grain can create deep scratches.) Wipe the surface clean with a tack cloth.

End cuts – where the wood is cut across the grain – may absorb a large quantity of stain, becoming darker than the rest of the furniture. If you don't want this effect, dilute some white shellac or other sealer to half its normal strength and brush it onto the open grain. When the sealer is dry, stain the edge.

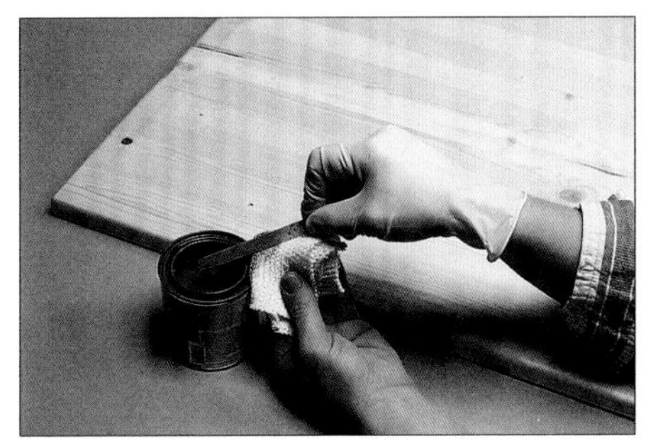

Using a wooden stir stick, stir the stain thoroughly. Wipe the stick on a rag and double check the color of the stain on the stick.

2 *Applying stain*

Lay the surface to be stained in a horizontal position to prevent runs. (If the furniture is heavy, get help lifting it.) Dip a brush or a rag into the stain and begin to spread the stain onto the wood. Most of the stain will be absorbed.

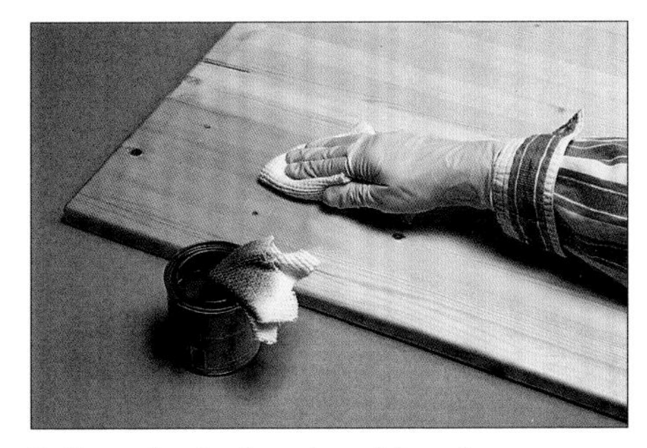

Follow the fresh stain with a clean rag, wiping away excess. Continue staining and wiping the excess, staining to the wet edge of the previous section.

When the full side is stained, allow to dry. Then turn it over and stain the other side. Continue until all sides of the piece are stained.

3 *Protecting the finish*

The finish of a stained piece must be protected. When the stained surfaces are dry, protect them by varnishing, oiling or waxing. To stencil or block print over a stained surface, varnish the stain first, or the paint will bleed into the grain of the wood. (See *Ivy League,* page 74.) Consult your paint store about the different applications available.

Clear thinking: Varnish in a dust-free setting.

Varnishing

Varnishing not only protects your paint job from scuffing, chipping and the effects of cleaning compounds. It also enriches color and gives a deep, glasslike finish. Some fragile materials such as paper and fabric, when protected by several coats of varnish, can be used in unexpected and creative ways. While it's best to apply varnish over an entire piece of furniture, you may opt to varnish only the parts that receive the most wear and need the greatest protection, such as a tabletop or the drawer fronts of a dresser.

Applying water-based varnish is like wrapping furniture in plastic, adding protection to your finish against scratches and scuffs.

Select a non-yellowing, water-based varnish in your choice of finish, from low luster to glossy. These varnishes are fast drying, skinning over within minutes, a quality that helps prevent dust from becoming embedded in the surface. Water-based varnishes have a relatively slight odor and are easy to clean up with soap and water.

There are only two rules for achieving water-based varnish perfection. First, do it fast, quickly "floating" the varnish onto the surface with a brush, never a roller. Second, resist the urge to touch. Varnish begins to set immediately, and brush marks, fingerprints and kitty's paw prints are permanent. When the varnish is dry (usually a few hours), sand the finish lightly with fine sandpaper, wipe clean with a tack cloth and apply another coat. Don't be alarmed by the cloudy effect sanding has on the varnish. It will disappear when the next coat is applied.

Occasionally, a project with a special treatment, such as crackled varnish, will call for an oil-based varnish. These varnishes take much longer to dry than water-based ones, overnight compared with a few hours. They also lend an amber tone to the finish.

MATERIALS

The following tools and materials may be required.

- easy-release painter's tape
- tack cloth
- quart (litre) non-yellowing, water-based varnish
- paint brush, 2 in. (5 cm) wide, for water-based paint
- fine sandpaper (220 grade or finer)
- paste wax or car wax, buffing cloth

1 *Getting started*

Use easy-release painter's tape to mask around the area that you will varnish. Varnish must be stirred, never shaken. Shaking will create a multitude of bubbles that become trapped in the quickly drying varnish. While applying the varnish, stir it about every fifteen minutes.

2 *Applying varnish*

With a tack cloth, wipe the piece to be varnished, removing every particle of dust from the surface.

Using the paint brush, apply the first coat. Dip your brush to a level about halfway up the bristles.

Without wiping the excess off the brush, flow on a short, wide strip of varnish, starting near one corner or edge. Brush varnish out quickly and smoothly in the direction of the length of the surface, not the width. Try to brush toward the edges. Brushing against edges causes runs and drips.

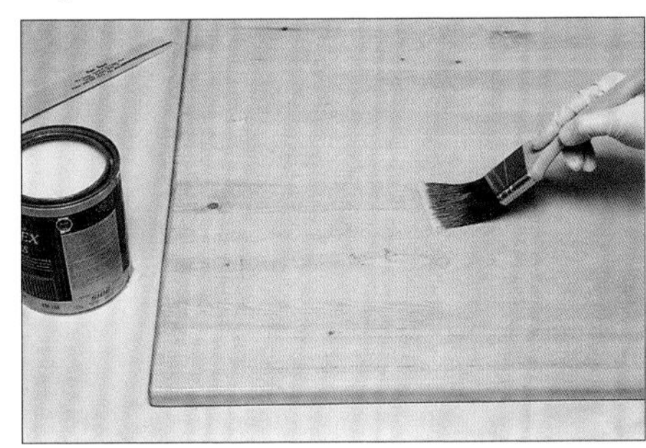

Repeat, brushing a second wide strip beside the first and connecting the strips. Continue until a section is complete. As you work, check for varnish that has slopped over edges and is creating drips. Wipe drips away with a brush, rag or finger. Continue across the surface, adding to the wet edge of previous strokes, until the surface is covered. Wash out the brush with soap and warm water.

Have a cup of tea and allow the varnish to dry.

3 *Additional coats*

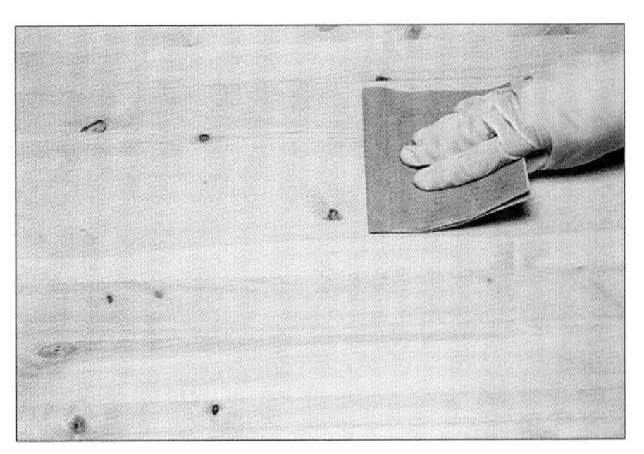

When the varnish is thoroughly dry (usually about a couple of hours), sand the first coat lightly with fine sandpaper and wipe thoroughly with a tack cloth. The cloudy effect that the sanding has on the varnish will disappear when you apply the next coat.

Apply a second coat. Allow to dry. Sand again and apply a third coat, if desired.

Optional: Applying and buffing a coat of paste wax or car wax over the last, dry coat of varnish will produce a glowing, buttery finish.

Crackled varnish is created by layering gum Arabic over tacky oil-based varnish. The resulting cracks are highlighted by thinned, rubbed-in brown oil paint.

Rustic Recipes

Crackle With A Side-order Of Potato Print

Crackle is reminiscent of weathered barns and farmhouse kitchens. Like pouring time from a bottle, applying this technique creates instant antiques. This time-worn, rural treatment of overlaid and crackled traditional colors is simply and quickly created with our easy recipe. Instant accents of diamonds and a sawtooth border are added by simple potato block-printing, which holds its own in any rustic setting.

Read This First

There are two types of crackle. One type has the effect of severely weathered paint. In the other, only the varnish is crazed into spiderweb-like cracks, while the underlying paint is intact. This project demonstrates the weathered-paint type of crackle. (For the second type, see page 55.) Pass over the pricey crackle kits sold in paint, art supply and craft stores. The inexpensive foolproof method demonstrated here creates incredibly authentic-looking crackle, quickly. To produce the crackle, a base-coat color of latex paint is applied to the furniture. If your cabinet has a plastic laminate finish, use melamine paint for the base coat. (See *Melamine Paint,* page 27.) This color will show through the cracks. Mucilage glue is brushed on over the paint. Then, while the glue is still wet, a coordinating top coat of paint is applied. This top coat will begin cracking within minutes. Latex-based paint cracks much more effectively than acrylic-based paint, although a latex-acrylic blend can be used. For this cabinet, strongly contrasting colors of paint were used to demonstrate the effect dramatically. Similar colors crackled overtop each other produce a subtle, intricate result.

Potato printing is a perfect complement for crackle. Potato prints are by nature simple and imperfect, uneven and semitransparent, with an aged look. Potato printing is as simple as it sounds – stamping with a cut-out potato, like a rubber stamp. (Also see *Lasting Impressions,* page 62.) Crackle, because it is so busy, can often obscure proportions and details. Potato printing or block printing accentuates details and restores order.

BEFORE

An intriguing cabinet of plank construction with a garage paint job of dull cement gray. Crackle and block printing will accentuate its 1920s vintage and its handsome proportions.

MATERIALS

- latex paint in two coordinating colors, 1 quart (litre) each (Choose a low-luster finish for authenticity.)
- mucilage glue, the amber type used in grade school (One bottle will cover a surface just larger than two of these books lying open.)
- inexpensive medium-sized paint brush (for glue)
- paint brush, 2 in. (5 cm) wide
- paper, pencil, scissors
- large potato
- sharp paring knife
- medium-sized artist's brush
- tubes of acrylics for potato print: cadmium red deep, mars black, yellow ochre
- ruler or tape measure

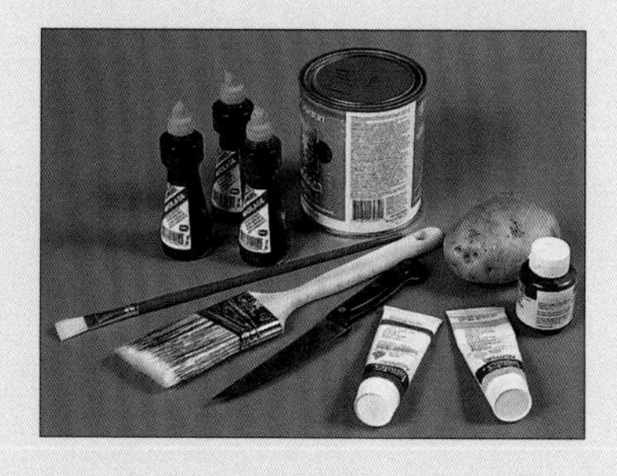

1 *Painting the base coat*

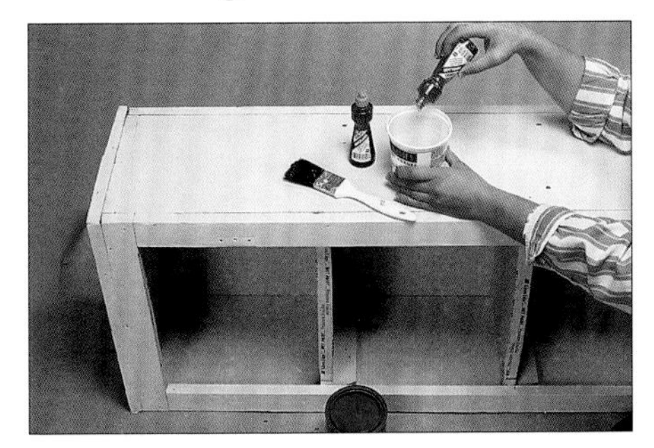

Refer to *Painting Basics* (page 34), and prepare and paint (priming is not necessary) the cabinet with the base-coat color. Apply two coats if necessary to achieve good coverage. This is the color that will show through the cracks. Allow the paint to dry. Place the area to be crackled in a horizontal position. (If the cabinet is heavy, get help moving it.) Decant some mucilage glue into a container.

2 *Applying crackle*

Apply the crackle in sections about 2 square feet (.2 m square). Using a medium-sized paint brush, spread the mucilage on the surface, brushing it out to a thin layer. The crackle will occur naturally along the direction of the brushstrokes. For busy, intricate crackle, brush in overlapping, multiple directions. Brush in straight lines for more even crackle. Place brush in glue and set aside.

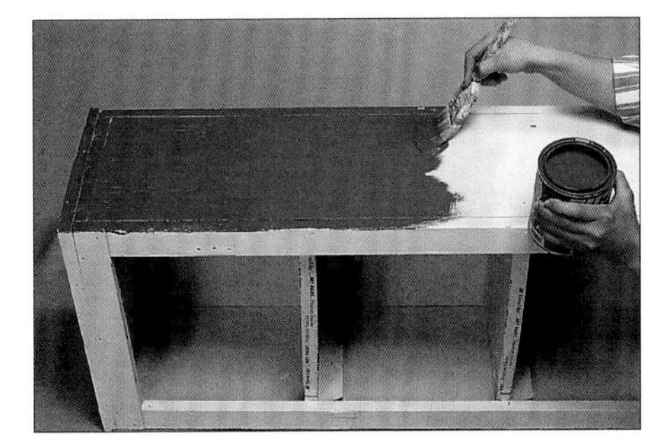

Without allowing the mucilage to dry, use the 2 in. (5 cm) paint brush and brush the second color of paint over the wet mucilage, almost to the edges of the glue. Flow the paint on without overbrushing. The largest crackles will be formed on the wettest glue, with the size of crackles diminishing as the paint is applied over damp glue. No crackles will be formed on dry glue.

Paint another section of glue, overlapping the still-wet edges of the first section, and apply more paint over the wet glue. Continue until the full side is covered. Cracking will start in minutes. Allow the side to dry. Continue crackling the cabinet until all sides are finished.

3 *Cutting the potato print*

Trace the pattern on page 55, or create your own pattern.

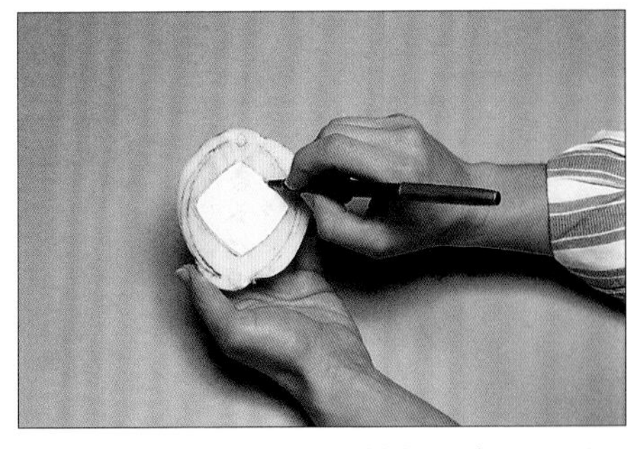

Cut a large potato in half, lengthwise. Cut out the design elements of the pattern and position them on the cut side of the potato-half. Trace around the pattern pieces with a pencil or a felt pen. (Retain the other potato-half.)

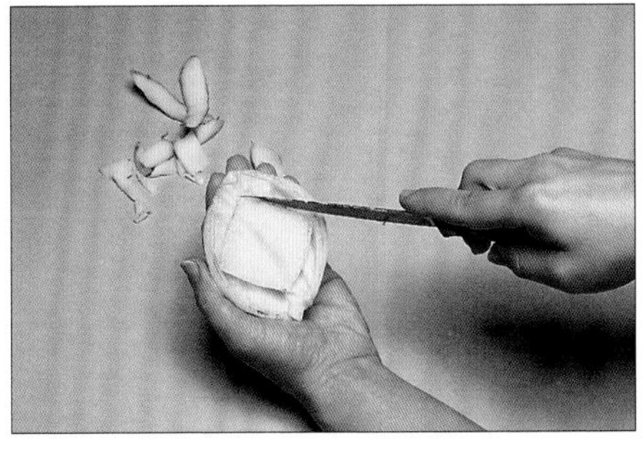

Using a sharp paring knife, cut away the potato surrounding the pattern outlines to a depth of about ¼ in. (.5 cm) or greater. On the uncarved side of the potato, carve two notches as a handle.

4 *Potato printing*

Using a medium-sized artist's brush, apply acrylics, in the desired colors, to the raised sections of the potato. (Shown here: cadmium red deep, mars black, and yellow ochre.)

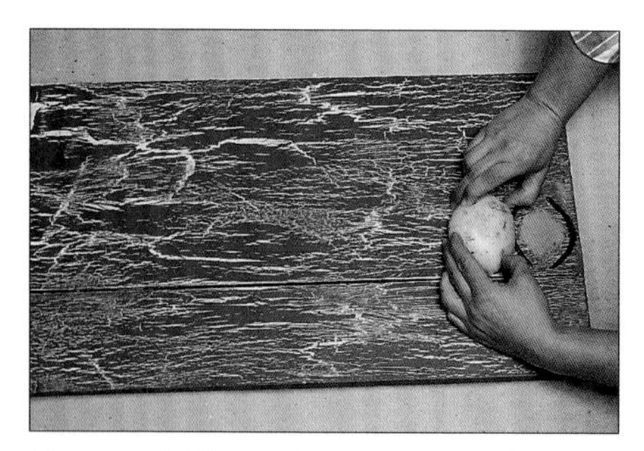

It's a good idea to do some test prints on paper before printing the cabinet. Carefully position the potato print, paint-side-down, onto the paper. Apply pressure so that the print makes full contact. Carefully lift the potato print off without sliding it. The print should be uneven and semitransparent, and it may have gaps.

Now place the surface to be printed in a horizontal position, so that you can apply pressure. Begin printing the cabinet, forming a border or a center design.

Continue printing with the potato, replenishing paint as needed, about every two or three prints. When finished, stand back and examine the prints. You can touch up any gaps or areas that are too transparent for your taste. Patting the paint on with a brush or your finger gives a block-printing effect.

5 *Sawtooth border*

To create a block-printed sawtooth border, cut an equilateral triangle (Geometry 101: all sides equal length) from the other potato-half. Measure and mark the center of the border. Apply mars black paint to the potato.

Position the first print on the center of the border, where marked. Work out from the center, with triangles just touching, until one edge of the border is complete.

Continue the border along adjoining sides, if desired.

Optional: Paint small motifs or dots in the open Vs of the sawtooth.

Attach the hardware.

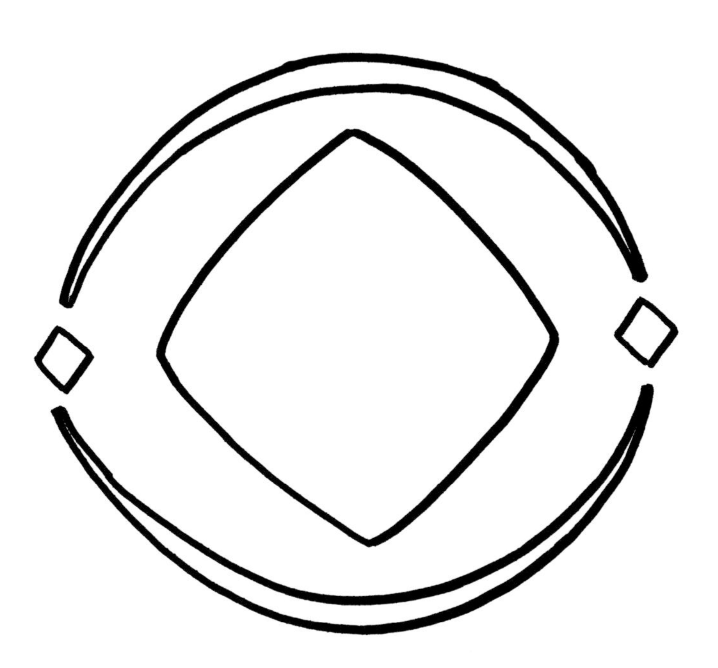

PATTERN FOR POTATO PRINT

For a more subtle, refined look than crackled paint, try creating crackled, antiqued varnish. Crackled varnish is created by layering gum Arabic over tacky oil-based varnish, then rubbing thinned, brown oil paint into the resulting cracks.

Prints Charming

Fluid, Fast Block Printing Adds Bedside Appeal

A large-scale, bold pattern adds both decoration and repetitive interest to a piece of furniture. And when the pattern is created with a block print it takes on a charming, distinctive folk and country feeling. Block printing is like cloth woven from natural fibers: it's not completely uniform. Each print is subtly different, adding a hand-crafted feeling. Block printing with a roller is a fast way to achieve an overall pattern. This technique eliminates the usual endless measuring and planning involved in creating uniform patterns.

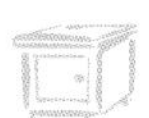

Read This First

This block-print treatment consists of two phases. First, the cabinet is painted with a base-coat color; then the print is applied with a roller. If your cabinet has a plastic laminate finish, use melamine paint for the base coat. (See *Melamine Paint,* page 27.) Purchase a small short-pile or foam roller and create the pattern to fit the roller. If the roller is much larger than the pattern, you'll find it hard to judge where the pattern should begin and end. The foam-printing blocks, which are laminated to the roller, can be cut from a foam insole. The insoles used for block printing should be the inexpensive kind, fabric on one side and perforated foam on the other. The small perforations will show up as tone-on-tone small dots. These dots give the design an additional decorative quality. Subtle changes occur from print to print as a result of variations in paint saturation and pressure. These slight differences should be viewed not as inconsistencies, but as desirable elements that create distinctive prints.

BEFORE

A 1960s-vintage bedstand that was acquired as part of a mismatched bedroom grouping. Its flat sides lend themselves perfectly to a block-printing treatment.

MATERIALS

- quart (litre) high-adhesion, water-based primer
- quart (litre) eggshell finish latex paint, cinnamon
- quart (litre) eggshell finish latex paint, cream
- painting tools: paint brush, small roller, roller tray
- paper (several large sheets), pencil, ruler, scissors
- pair of inexpensive foam insoles
- spray glue
- paper towels
- medium-sized artist's brush
- quart (litre) non-yellowing, water-based varnish
- *optional:* chalk or erasable pencil

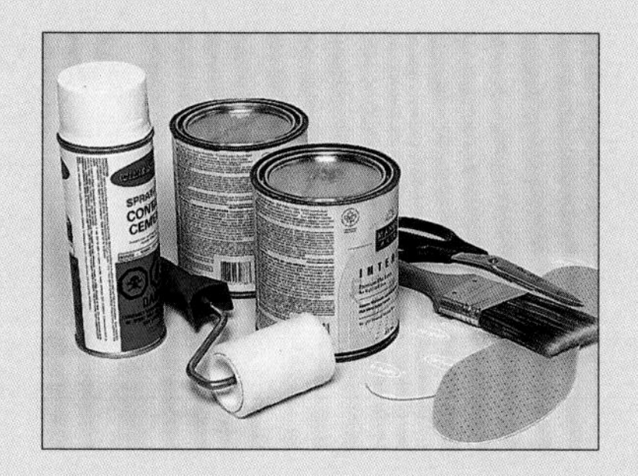

1 *Painting the base coat*

Refer to *Painting Basics* (page 34). Prepare and prime the cabinet before painting it with two coats of latex paint. The body of this cabinet is painted cinnamon and the doors cream.

2 *Cutting the block print*

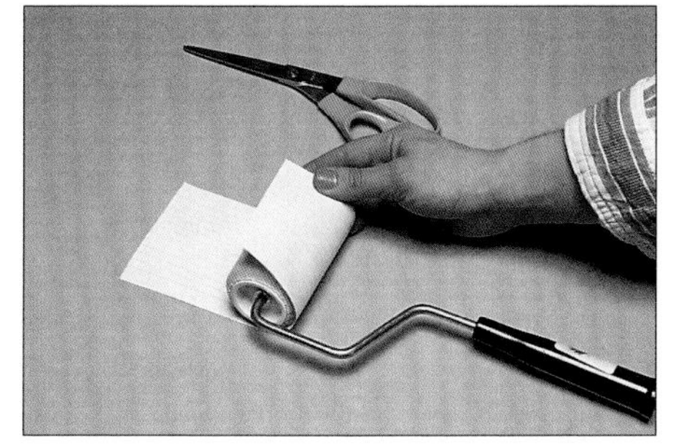

Begin making a pattern for the block print. Cut a strip of paper the width of the roller. Wrap the paper around the roller until the ends meet. Mark and cut the paper to this length. The paper should now fit neatly around the roller. Measure the piece of paper and set aside the measurements.

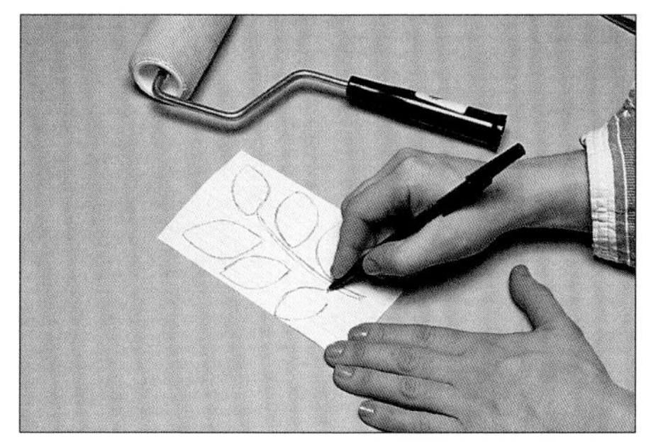

Trace the pattern from page 60, or draw a design, onto the pattern paper. A simple design is best.

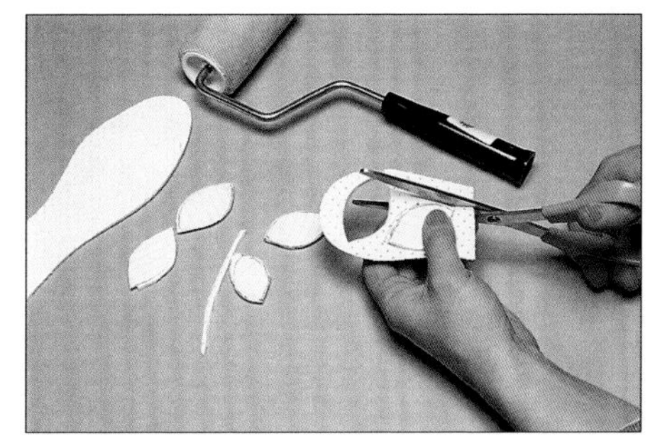

Cut out the paper pattern pieces. One by one, lay a pattern piece onto the insole and cut around it until all pieces are cut out.

Note: Positioning the pattern for cutting on the fabric side of the insole will print the pattern as you drew it. Cutting from the foam side will print the image in reverse.

3 *Laminating the block print*

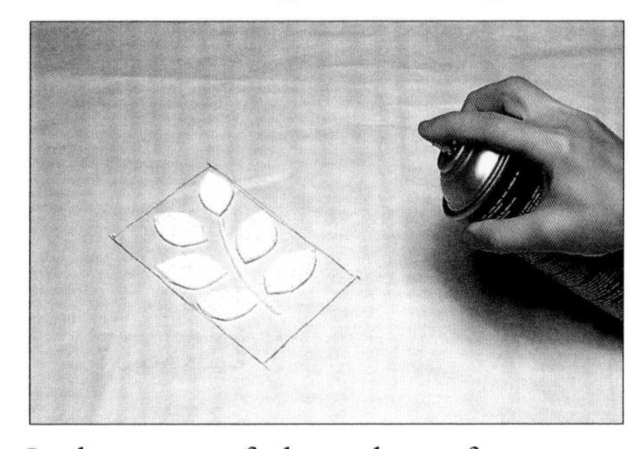

In the center of a large sheet of paper, draw a rectangle to match the pattern paper (from step 2). The excess paper is needed to catch oversparay from the spray glue.

Lay the foam pieces *foam-side-down* within the rectangle's outline. Feel free to move pieces around and alter the original design.

Read the instructions on the spray-glue can for making a permanent bond. Usually the label states that the bond must be made when the glue is still "aggressively tacky," which means to spray, wait about two minutes, then bond the surfaces. Spray the fabric side of the foam pieces well with the glue.

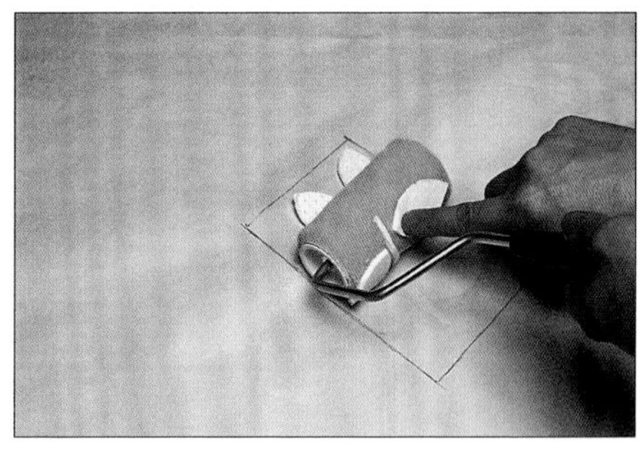

Position the roller on the paper at the base of the rectangle's outline, then begin slowly rolling it over the pattern pieces, lifting them and sticking them to the roller as you go. Don't worry if glue gets onto the roller fuzz. It will dry.

4 *Test printing*

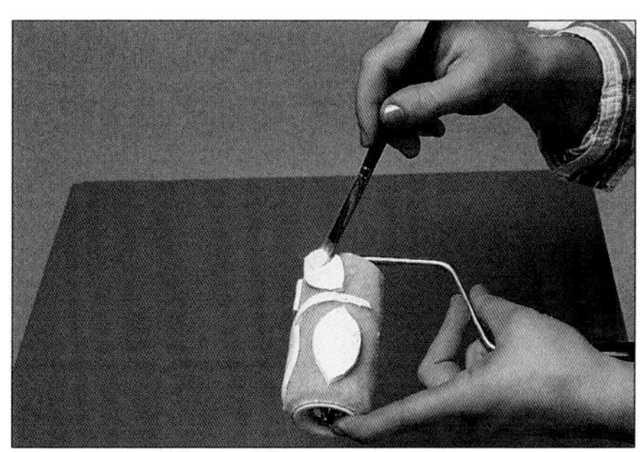

Slightly dampen the foam pieces with a wet paper towel. With the artist's brush, apply paint onto the foam sections, using a color that contrasts with the painted background. Avoid getting paint onto the roller fuzz. The paint should flow easily, but it should not be watery. Before printing on the furniture, make some tests on paper to get the hang of the technique. Often, the foam prints better after several passes.

5 *Printing furniture*

Position the cabinet so that the side to be printed is horizontal. (If the cabinet is heavy, get some help turning it.) Before printing the furniture, you may wish to draw a chalk line to follow for printing. Or you can visualize a line, such as corner to corner (as was done on this cabinet). Follow the line with either the side edge or the center of the roller. Apply paint to the foam patterns. Position the roller at the beginning of the chalk (or imaginary) line, making sure the base of the pattern is at the starting point. Smoothly roll the image to the end of the line, applying even pressure.

Repeat a second line of patterns. Subsequent lines of pattern can be staggered, or the roller can be flopped (flipped over) to produce alternate upside-down rows. Allow to dry. Wash out the foam patterns, pat dry and print a second color if desired.

6 *Finishing*

Enrich the color and protect the paint by applying one or more coats of non-yellowing, water-based varnish. (See *Varnishing*, page 48.)

Attach the hardware.

PATTERN FOR BLOCK PRINT

Roller block printing works well in combination with other techniques. Shown here, block printing over stained wood with a border of patinated copper. (See Ivy League, page 74.)

Lasting Impressions

A Simple, Striking School Of Block-Printed Fish

Country-blue fish on an off-white background perpetually swim the perimeter of a generously proportioned round table. Each block-printed fish is unique and decorative. Uncomplicated yet irresistible, the freshness of a block print can never be matched by painting with a brush. A potato-print sawtooth border completes a design that combines rustic simplicity with a bold and stylish touch.

Read This First

This project utilizes one of the easiest paint techniques: block printing. Patterns are cut from an insole (the foam insert that goes into your shoe) and a potato, then easily applied. Printing with a foam insole may seem unusual, but the small regular pinholes give a decorative effect, and the composition of the insole makes it easy to cut, to carve details into and to manipulate. Dependable potato printing, in which a carved potato is used like a rubber stamp, is ideal for small designs and patterns. Before the block printing is done, the table is painted with a solid base-coat color of latex paint. If your table has a plastic laminate finish, use melamine paint. (See *Melamine Paint,* page 27.) Block printing can also be effective on natural wood that has been stained and varnished with one coat. Varnish again after the block printing.

BEFORE

Used for a stage set, this solid wood table, painted overpowering green in a heavy enamel, was chipped and peeling. It called for a simple, fresh treatment.

MATERIALS

- quart (litre) high-adhesion, water-based primer
- quart (litre) eggshell or satin finish latex paint, off-white
- 1 pint (.5 litre) latex paint, Wedgwood or linen blue
- painting tools: paint brush, small roller, roller tray
- access to photocopier, or paper and pencil
- permanent waterproof marker
- inexpensive foam insoles
- scissors, X-acto knife
- paper
- easy-release painter's tape
- inexpensive square-tipped artist's brush
- large potato
- sharp paring knife
- quart (litre) non-yellowing, water-based varnish
- *optional:* spray primer; low-luster acrylic spray primer

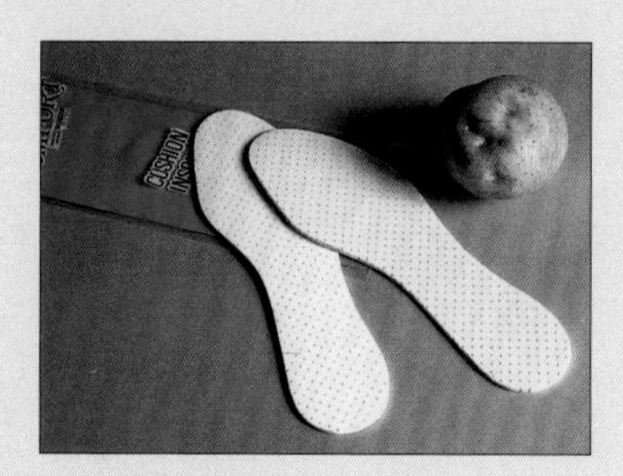

1 *Painting*

Refer to *Painting Basics* (page 34). Prepare, prime and paint the table and chairs with the off-white latex paint. Spray primer and paint may be used on the table base and chairs. (See *Spray Painting*, page 44.) The base of the table can be painted blue, if desired.

2 *Making the fish block print*

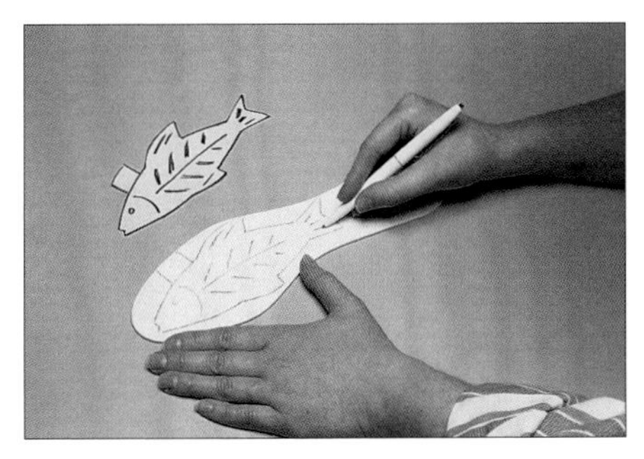

Photocopy the fish pattern (page 67) to an appropriate size for your table. (You could also trace the pattern using paper and pencil.) Keep in mind that the pattern must fit onto the insole. Cut out the pattern.

Position the pattern onto the foam side of the insole and trace around it (including the tab) with a permanent waterproof marker. The fish, when printed, will be swimming in the opposite direction of the pattern. (If you wish the fish to swim in the same direction as the pattern, place the pattern on the cloth side.)

Cut along the outline of the fish, including the tab. Draw the detail lines on the foam side of the fish.

3 *Adding detail*

Create scales, gills and other details in the fish. Using the X-acto knife, score two parallel cuts close together along the lines on the foam. Cut the foam, but don't cut through the fabric backing. Scrape the foam off the fabric backing between the parallel cuts. Remove a dot of foam for the eye. Score through the foam (not the fabric backing) at the base of the tab, so that it can bend back easily.

4 *Planning prints*

Cut several fish from paper and position them onto the tabletop in the direction they will print, spacing them evenly apart. Tape the paper fish lightly in place using easy-release painter's tape. Other tape may lift your paint.

5 *Test printing*

Test the fish print on some paper before printing the table. Using a square-tipped artist's brush, brush the blue paint onto the foam side of the fish, avoiding the tab. Place the fish foam-side-down onto the paper. Press gently all over the fabric side of the fish, being certain that it has made full contact. Lifting the tab, peel the fish from the paper.

Every print will be different. Applying more paint to the foam will make a darker print, with less detail. (Excess paint floods details, obscuring them.) Less paint gives a paler effect, with crisper detail. Make several test prints from one load of paint on the foam. Most block prints give better results after some use.

6 *Printing*

Begin to print the table. Apply paint to the foam. Then lift one paper pattern, placing the fish foam-side-down in place of the pattern.

Press fish evenly all over, then peel off. After several prints, paint may seep through the fabric backing. Although seepage is not a problem for the printing, be careful not to transfer paint from your hands to the tabletop.

Don't forget the chairs! Print as desired. Two fish, back-to-back on the seat or across the backrest, will coordinate the pieces.

7 *Making the potato print*

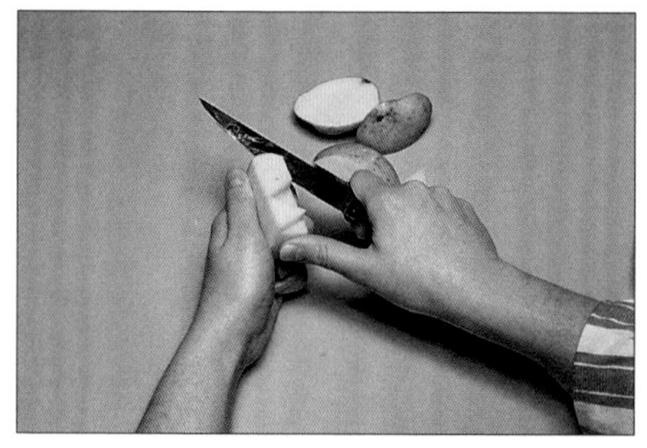

Make a sawtooth pattern around the table's edge. Use the paring knife to carve a solid W pattern (or use the pattern on page 67 as a guide) into a block of potato. To help you place the image when printing, cut away excess potato around the W, but leave enough attached to the back for a handle.

8 *Potato printing*

Make some test prints on paper. Brush some paint onto the W and press onto the paper, using a rocking motion.

Begin printing a continuous sawtooth around the edge of the table. Brush paint onto the W. Position the wide edge of the W against the outside edge of the table.

Press the image firmly down in a rocking motion toward the center of the table. Position each print tightly against the previous one to line up the pattern evenly.

When you are several sawtooth prints away from the end, you may wish to cut the W print in half and print each V individually. Overlap or spread the prints apart slightly to fill the remaining space as evenly as possible. Add sawtooth to the chairs if desired.

9 *Additional prints*

Add any further pattern or design, if desired. Here, a second potato print of three small leaves (see pattern, page 67) was added between the fish.

10 *Varnishing*

To enrich color and protect the paint, apply one or more coats of non-yellowing, water-based varnish to the tabletop, the chair seats and the backrests. (See *Varnishing*, page 48.)

FISH BLOCK-PRINT PATTERN

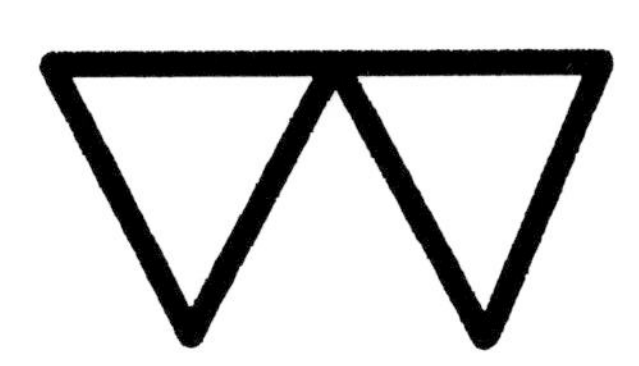

SAWTOOTH POTATO-PRINT PATTERN

THREE-LEAF POTATO-PRINT PATTERN

Vanity Flair

Give Them The Moon And The Stars With Unique Reverse-Stencils

String a milky way of magical copper-gold stars and moons on a suedelike painted background to enchant a bedroom. These universally favored motifs, placed at random, give any dated furniture, especially dressers or vanities, an opulent and contemporary sensibility. The foil-like quality of a brushed-on metallic galaxy provides a glowing counterpoint to a soft, sponge-painted background in hazy tones of blue or sand.

Read This First

Traditional stenciling techniques give you a uniform, smooth coat of paint. To obtain a more brush-painted effect, use a reverse-stenciling technique. The color (copper) of the stenciled image is painted in position first. Then, self-adhesive cut-out images (decals) of moons and stars are stuck onto the copper paint. The base-coat color is painted and sponge painted over the moon and star decals and the surrounding area. Finally, the decals are removed to reveal brush-painted motifs that provide a perfect counterpoint to the soft, sponge-painted background. Sponge painting furniture differs from sponging a wall. The technique is similar, but the scale is much smaller. Try to find a natural or synthetic sponge that has small pores to give you a less ragged, more refined texture. And while the motif of the moon and stars is a universal favorite, ideal for this stenciling technique, many other simple shapes will work nicely too. (Patterns for the stencils are on page 73.)

Before

A 1950s waterfall-style dresser set, but without the beautiful inlay of the better-quality dressers and vanities of its era. Instead, this set was covered in a peculiar bumpy finish made from a sprayed-on resinlike product.

Materials

- quart (litre) high-adhesion, water-based primer
- painting tools: paint brush, small roller, roller tray
- easy-release painter's tape, 2 in. (5 cm) wide
- marker and scissors
- tubes of acrylics, iridescent copper and gold
- inexpensive, medium-sized square-tipped artist's brush
- quart (litre) eggshell finish latex paint, off-white (step 4)
- quart (litre) eggshell finish latex paint, taupe
- tubes of acrylics, raw sienna and yellow oxide
- flat containers for paints
- synthetic or natural sponge for sponge painting
- X-acto knife
- fine-point artist's brush
- quart (litre) non-yellowing, water-based varnish
- *optional:* pint (.5 litre) latex paint, slate blue
- *optional:* tubes of acrylics, Payne's gray and pthalo blue

1 *Priming*

Refer to *Painting Basics* (page 34). Prepare and prime, but *do not paint* the dresser.

2 *Cutting reverse-stencil decals*

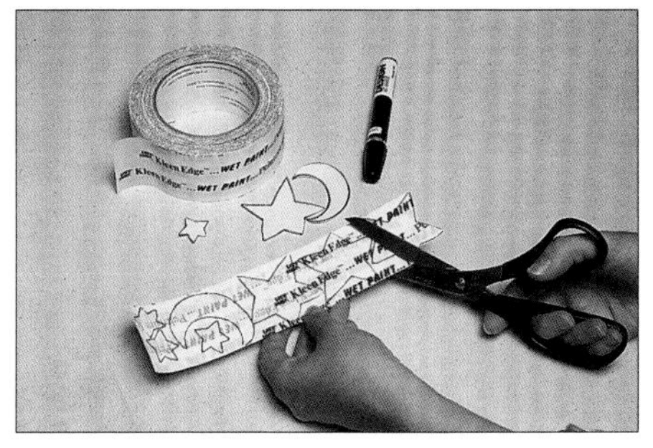

Trace the patterns on page 73 onto a piece of easy-release painter's tape. Cut five pieces of tape and layer them, sticking the pattern tracings on top. Cut out the patterns, through all layers of tape. Set the decals aside. You won't know exactly how many decals you will need until you apply them to the dresser.

3 *Placing reverse-stencil decals*

With the drawers in place in the dresser, paint sites for the moon and star motifs by brushing patches in a random pattern onto the dresser, using the square-tipped artist's brush and the copper and gold acrylics. Rather than mixing the colors, take some paint from each tube directly onto the brush. Brushstrokes are desirable. Check that the patches are large enough to accommodate the moon and stars decals. Allow to dry.

One by one, stick the decals onto the copper and gold patches, until each patch has a decal. Cut more decals if needed.

4 *Painting*

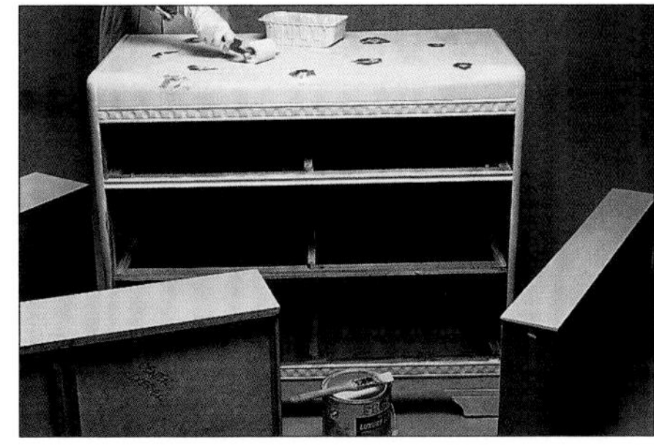

Note: The instructions are for painting the background a tan shade. For a stormy-blue background, substitute the optional blue and gray paints. (See step 7.)

Refer to *Painting Basics* (page 34). Using the paint brush and roller and the off-white latex paint, paint the dresser with one coat of paint, painting over the moon and stars decals. Get as much coverage as possible with this coat. This will be the base coat. When sponge painting, the base-coat color is the one that shows the least. Allow to dry.

Note: If painting the interiors of drawers, give them a second coat. If you do not wish to sponge paint the dresser, apply a second coat of off-white paint and remove the decals when the paint is dry to the touch, but still soft. Go to step 8.

5 *Sponge painting*

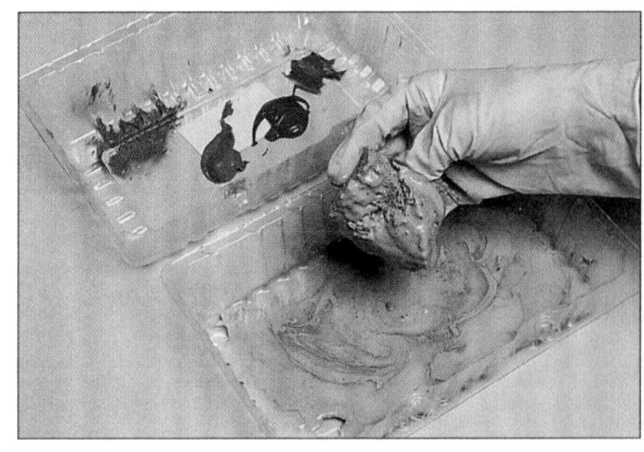

Starting on the top, sponge paint the dresser in sections. Begin sponging when the latex paint is dry to the touch. Pour some taupe latex paint into a flat container. In another container, squeeze a mound each of raw sienna and yellow oxide acrylics. Glaze and extender may be added to the paint, if desired. (For information, see *Glaze* and *Extender,* page 28.) Tear off a chunk from the sponge, about the size of a tennis ball. Dampen it slightly with water, then dip it into the taupe paint. Saturate the sponge, then wring out some of the excess.

With a small pouncing motion, sponge the taupe over the surface, allowing about 50% of the base coat to show through. Always use a pouncing or patting motion. Avoid dragging the sponge.

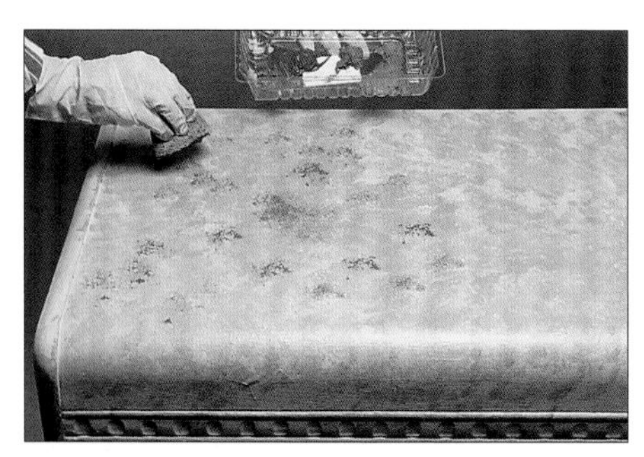

While the taupe is still damp, dip the sponge into the raw sienna and yellow oxide acrylics, picking up both colors. Sponge these paints over the taupe.

Sponging with only a few pounces will create a coarse pattern. The more pouncing and sponging, the more subtle, blended and suedelike the effect, especially if you're sponging onto still-damp paint.

6 *Sponge painting, continued*

With the drawers in place in the dresser (or remove the drawers and line them up in order, so that the pattern is continuous), repeat step 5, sponge painting the drawers.

Remove the decals while the paint is dry to the touch but still soft. Use the point of an X-acto knife to lift an edge, and then peel off the decal.

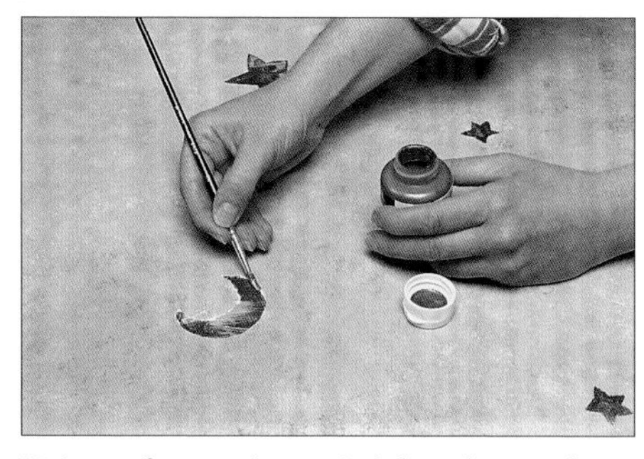

Using a fine-point artist's brush, touch up any areas where the sponging may have seeped under the decals.

7 *Painting trim*

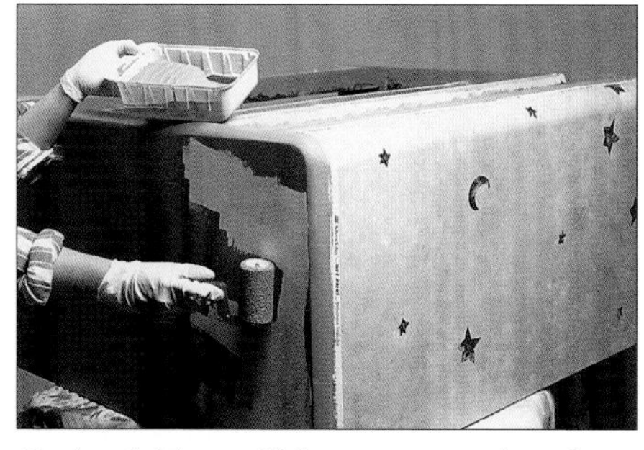

Optional: Tape off the sponge-painted areas and paint the trim with a base coat of slate blue latex paint. For a stormy-sky look, sponge paint the base coat with Payne's gray and pthalo blue acrylics.

8 *Varnishing*

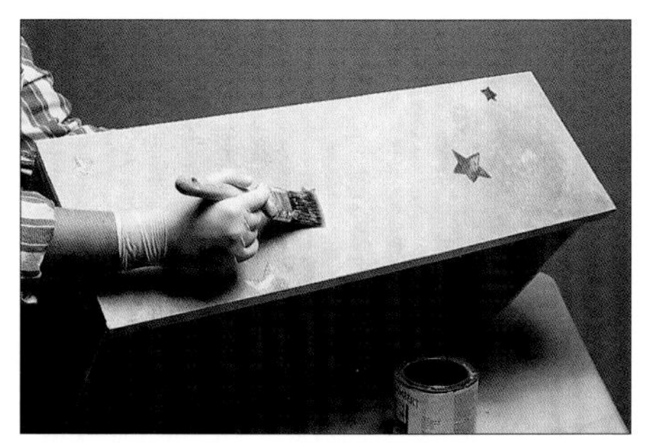

Enrich the color and protect the paint with one or more coats of non-yellowing, water-based varnish. (See *Varnishing*, page 48.)

PATTERNS FOR REVERSE-STENCILING DECALS

Ernest & Julio
FRENCH

Ivy League

Set An Amber-Stained Table With Ivy Trimmed In Copper

Mix some natural elements – natural wood burnished by a honey stain, trailing vines laden with leaves in rich summer greens, and copper ore weathered to a glorious patina. These are the types of elements meant to be combined. They offset each other while creating harmony in texture and tone, resulting in a remarkable piece of furniture.

Read This First

Choose a wooden table that is unpainted, or one that has a thoroughly stripped wooden tabletop. The tabletop is stained, and stain must be applied to raw wood. (The table's base can be made of any material.) A copper border is then painted and patinated. The vines and ivy leaves are block printed with a roller – a fast, easy method – and additional leaves are added at random for spontaneity. Then the whole top is varnished. The base of the table is painted deep teal green with latex paint. If your table base has a plastic laminate finish, use melamine paint. (See *Melamine Paint,* page 27.) Finally, the table is assembled. Although each phase of the process is simple and straightforward, the results are outstanding. The copper (often called copper topper) for the border and the patina (choose blue or green) can be purchased at art supply or craft stores. Purchase the compatible primer-sealer as well.

MATERIALS

- quart (litre) high-adhesion, water-based primer
- quart (litre) eggshell finish latex paint, deep teal green
- paint brush, 1½ in. (4 cm) wide
- ½ pint (250 ml) amber stain
- quart (litre) non-yellowing, water-based varnish
- ruler or tape measure
- easy-release painter's tape
- small boxes or plastic containers for supporting tabletop
- paint-on ground copper; compatible liquid patina (blue or green); clear, compatible primer-sealer
- 4 in. (10 cm) roller with sleeve
- several sheets of paper
- pair of inexpensive foam insoles
- pen or pencil
- scissors, X-acto knife
- spray glue; scrap paper or dropsheet
- light-colored pencil or piece of chalk
- fine-point artist's brush
- acrylic glazes (or mix acrylics and glaze, or substitute transparent acrylic paint), deep green, medium green, light green
- square-tipped artist's brush

BEFORE

A knockdown table of unpainted solid wood. The possibilities for creative finishing are endless.

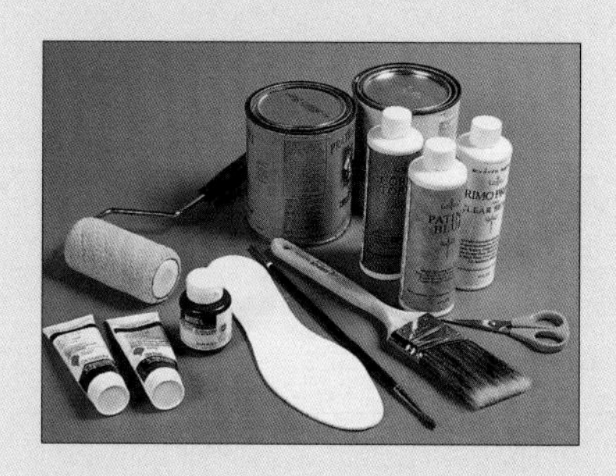

1 *Painting*

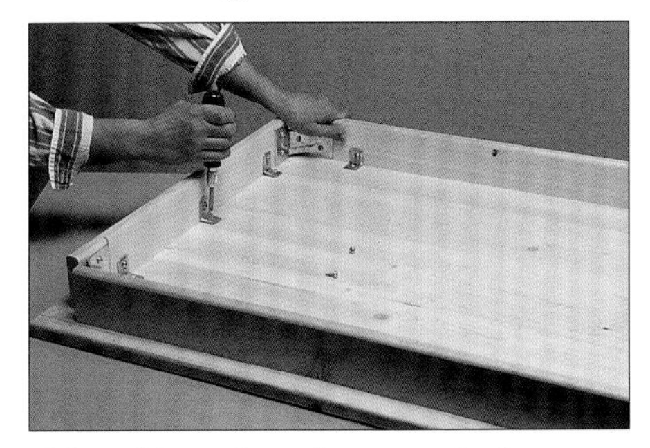

If the tabletop has a base attached, use the appropriate tools and remove it, if possible.

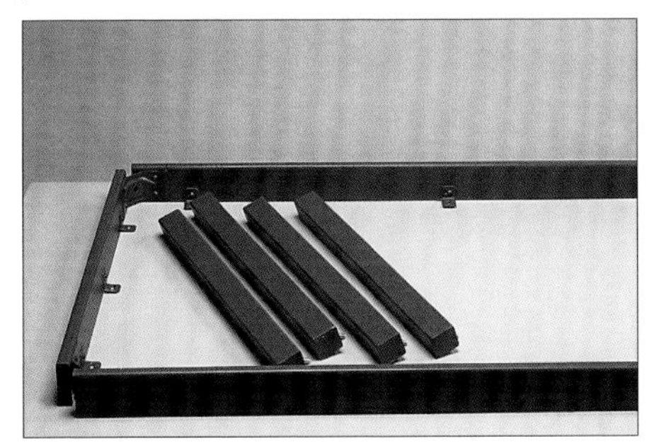

Refer to *Painting Basics* (page 34). Prepare, prime and paint the base and the legs deep teal green. Allow to dry. If your table is wooden and you wish to antique the base, do not prime it before painting.

2 *Staining and varnishing*

Stain the tabletop on both sides with the amber stain. Stain the underside first, then stain the top and sides. (See *Staining Wood,* page 46.)

Apply a coat of non-yellowing, water-based varnish (or the clear primer-sealer for the copper) to the underside, the top and the sides of the tabletop. The varnish will protect the stained wood, making it easy to wipe off any marks you might make while working. (See *Varnishing,* page 48.)

3 *Copper border*

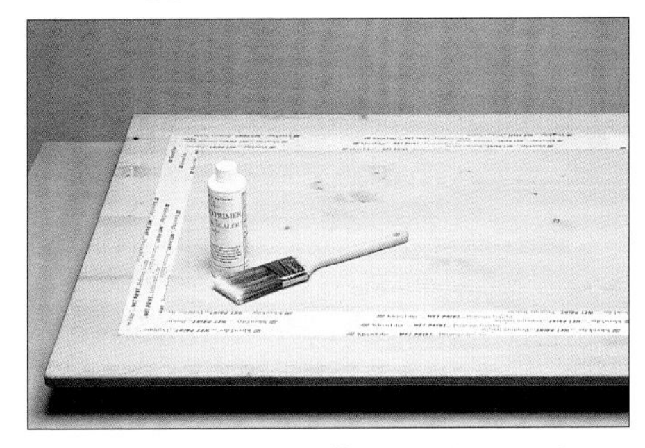

Measure and mask off a 3 in. (7.5 cm) wide border around the edge of the tabletop with easy-release painter's tape. Mask an equivalent border on the underside of the table. The underside will be done first. Support the tabletop, upside-down, on small boxes or plastic containers.

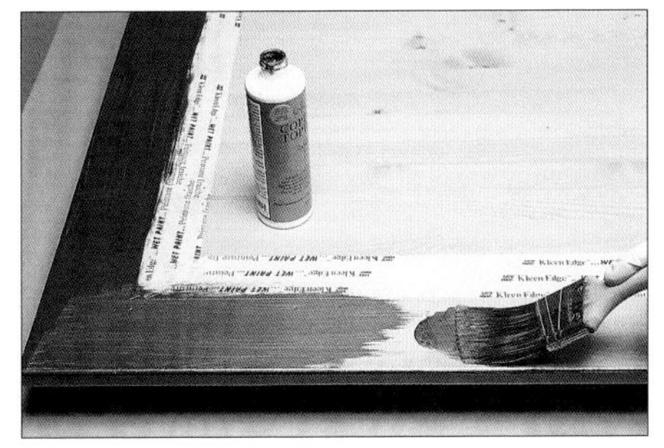

Paint the border and the edges with the ground copper (copper topper). When the copper topper is dry to the touch, turn the table over and paint the border on the top. Read the manufacturer's instructions for the copper and apply a second coat, if recommended. Allow to dry.

Pour some patina blue (or green) into a small container. Brush the patina onto the copper on the underside of the table. Allow it to start turning color, then turn the tabletop over and apply the patina to the remaining copper on the top side and the edges.

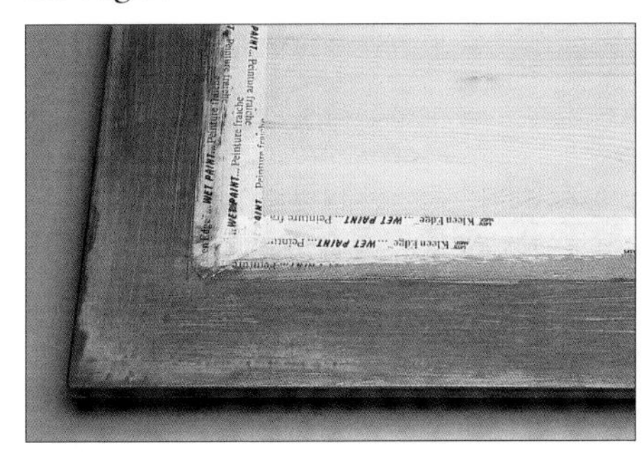

The patina will begin coloring the copper very quickly; however, it must cure fully before being coated with primer-sealer, often taking three days. Read the manufacturer's instructions. Allow the patina to cure fully, then coat the copper border with clear, compatible primer-sealer. Allow to dry and remove all tape.

Apply a coat of primer-sealer to the patinated copper border on both sides of the tabletop. Do the underside of the table first. Coating the full tabletop will prevent a ridge of sealer from forming along the edge of the border. Allow to dry.

4 *Cutting patterns*

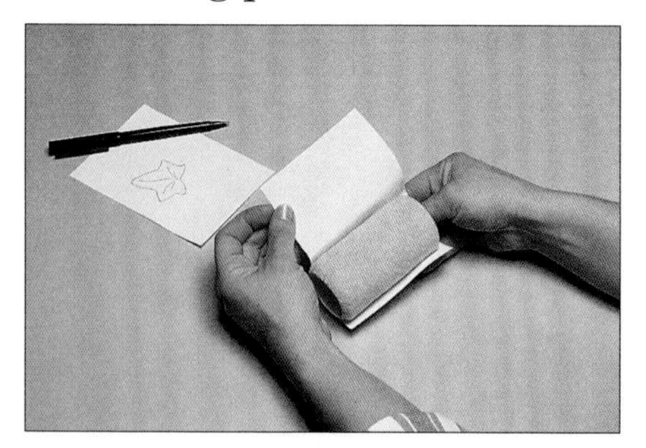

Trace the pattern for the *Small Ivy Leaf*, below. Set it aside. Cut a piece of paper the width of the roller sleeve and the right length to wrap around the sleeve.

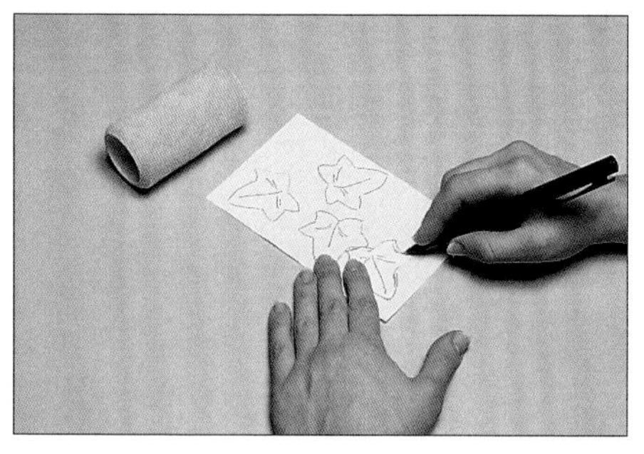

Determine how many ivy leaves you will need. Cut out the traced ivy leaf. Trace around the leaf, onto the paper that fits around the roller. Make several tracings, creating a pattern of leaves along the length of the paper. Set this paper aside.

Small Ivy Leaf Pattern

5 *Cutting block prints*

Lay the cut-out leaf pattern on the cloth side of an insole and trace around it. Continue tracing the pattern until you have the required number of ivy leaves. Cut out the leaves with scissors.

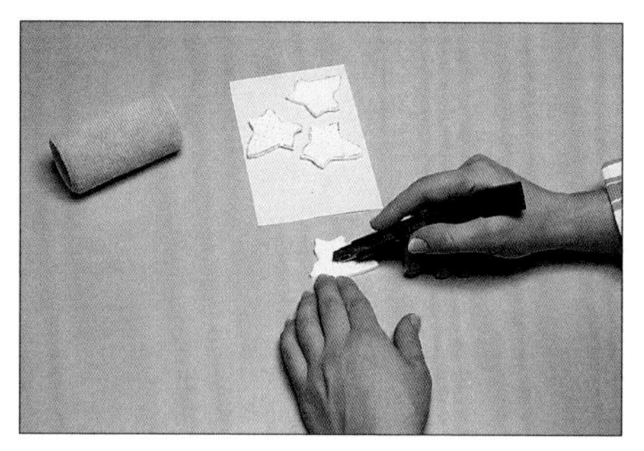

Using the X-acto knife, score veins into the leaves, cutting the foam – but not all the way through the cloth backing. As each leaf is finished, lay it *foam-side-down* onto the roller-sized piece of paper. You may wish to position the leaves as you originally placed and indicated them, or you could turn the paper over (to eliminate your original layout) and rearrange the pattern.

6 *Gluing block prints*

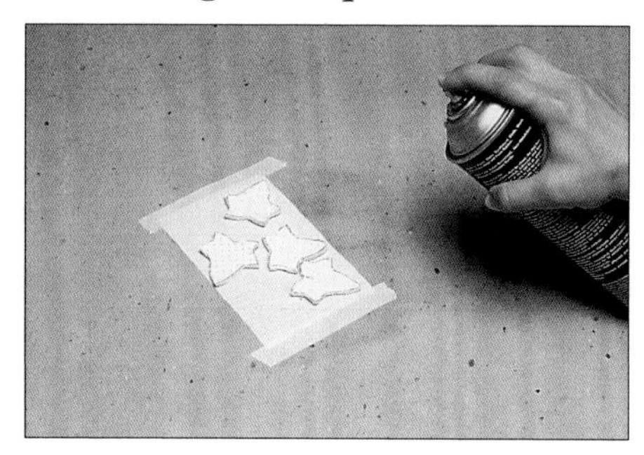

Position the roller-sized paper (with the ivy leaves on it) onto some scrap paper to catch any overspray from the glue.

Tape the edges down. Read the instructions on the spray-glue can for making a permanent bond. Most say to attach surfaces when the glue is "aggressively tacky," which means to spray, wait about two minutes, and then bond the surfaces. Check that the leaves are foam-side-down, then spray with glue.

Position the roller sleeve straight, at one end of the paper. Slowly roll the sleeve over the paper, picking up the foam leaves. Assist by lifting the leaves with your fingers if necessary. Don't worry if some glue becomes attached to the roller fuzz. It will dry. Continue until all leaves are securely glued to the roller sleeve. Set aside.

7 *Painting vines*

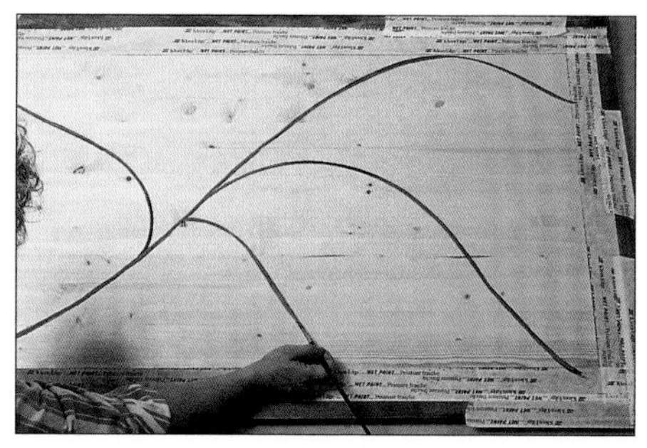

Using easy-release painter's tape, mask off the copper border. With a light shade of colored pencil or a piece of chalk, draw vines onto the center of the table. Make the lines gently curved so they will be easy to follow with the roller. Thin some medium-green paint or use a glaze to paint the vines. The paint should flow freely from a fine-point artist's brush. Paint the lines quickly, using your sketched lines only as a guide. Allow to dry.

8 *Printing*

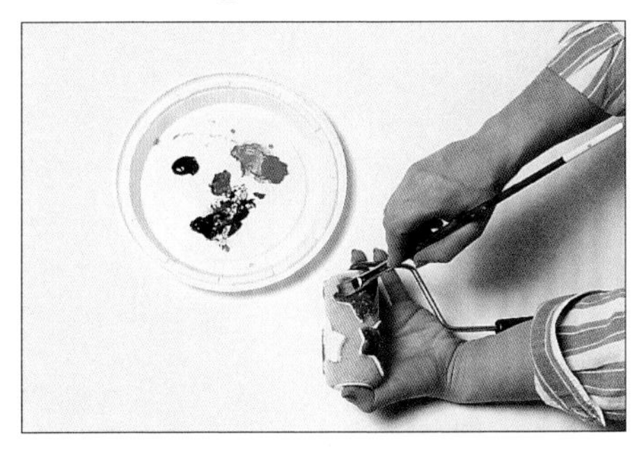

Do some roller-print tests on paper before rolling the table. Apply paint to the foam leaves by painting them with a square-tipped artist's brush and several shades of green glaze, or transparent acrylic paint thinned with water. For greater depth and interest, try painting more than one shade of green on a leaf. Avoid getting paint on the roller fuzz. Lay the roller on the paper and apply pressure as you roll. Generally the block prints are better and crisper, with more detail, after some use.

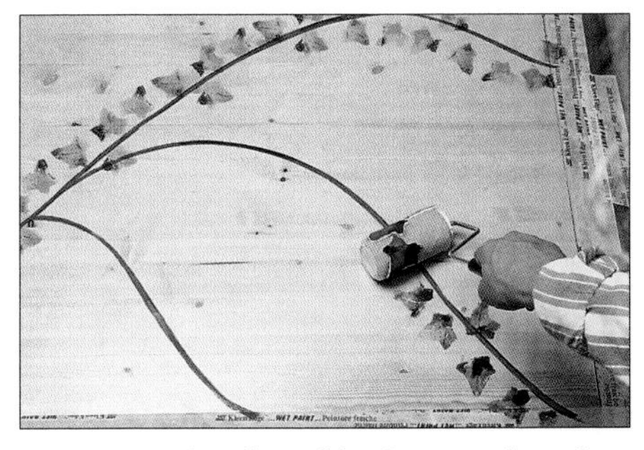

Begin to print the table. Start at the edge of the table and roll into the center, following a vine. Try to keep the vine in the center of the roller as you roll, stopping at the junction of another vine or at the table edge. Continue adding paint to the foam and printing until all vines have leaves.

9 *Finishing touches*

Optional: If your pattern appears too regular for your liking, add some random large ivy leaves. Trace the *Large Ivy Leaf* pattern (this page), including the tab. Transfer it to the cloth side of the insole and cut out the shape. Score veins into the foam side and score between the tab and the leaf. Use this foam leaf as a single block print.

Apply paint to the foam side except for the tab, and apply the print to the tabletop, pressing it evenly. Remove the foam leaf by lifting it by its tab. Add leaves along the vines, as desired. These larger leaves can overlap the smaller ones.

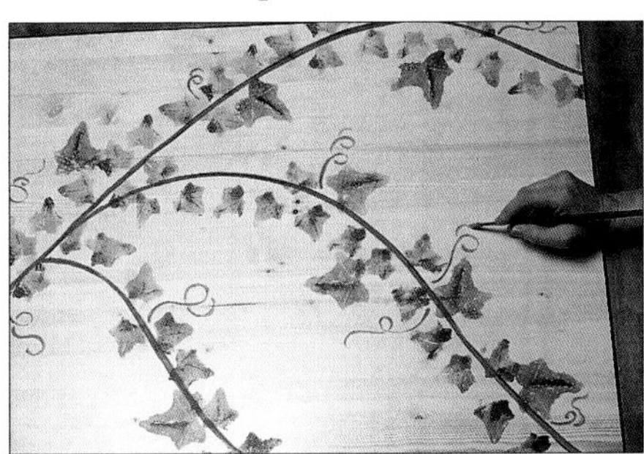

Optional: Using the fine-point artist's brush and some paint or glaze, paint freehand tendrils randomly along the vines. A narrow border may also be masked and painted along the edge of the copper border.

10 *Varnishing*

Enrich color and protect the stained wood and your paint job by varnishing the tabletop and edges with two coats of non-yellowing, water-based varnish. (See *Varnishing,* page 48.) Allow to dry.

11 *Finishing*

Reassemble the base of the table with the top.

LARGE IVY LEAF PATTERN

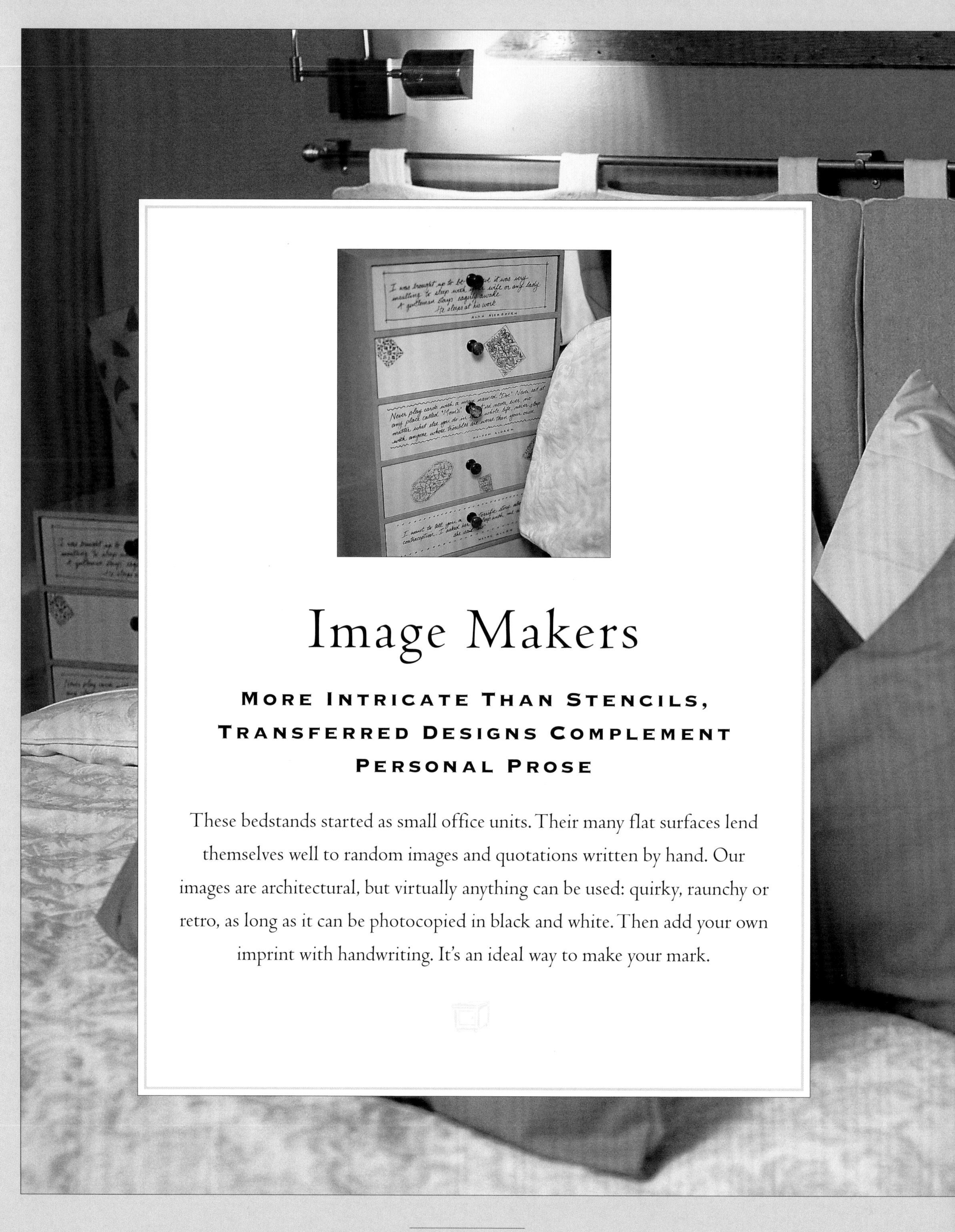

Image Makers

More Intricate Than Stencils, Transferred Designs Complement Personal Prose

These bedstands started as small office units. Their many flat surfaces lend themselves well to random images and quotations written by hand. Our images are architectural, but virtually anything can be used: quirky, raunchy or retro, as long as it can be photocopied in black and white. Then add your own imprint with handwriting. It's an ideal way to make your mark.

Sleep is when all the
stuff comes flying
out as from a dustbin upset in a high wind.
WILLIAM GOLDING
She's invented a
religion called
'Creative Sleep.'
HENRY REED
with her feet resting upon
dreams and a
hue.

Read This First

This project consists of only two techniques, handwriting and photo transfer, over a base coat of paint, but it looks like many more. If your furniture has a plastic laminate finish, use melamine paint for the base coat. (See *Melamine Paint,* page 27.) Choose quotations on any subject for the handwriting, perhaps from a book of modern quotations available at the local library or bookstore. If you have reservations about writing on a piece of furniture, keep in mind that it's not the perfection of your script that counts. On the contrary, your unique style is what makes the piece so personal and original.

As a counterpoint to the script, images are photocopied and then transferred onto alternating drawers and in open areas. The transfer is achieved by burnishing the wrong side of the photocopy with a broad nib marker, or turpentine. The chemicals melt the photocopy ink and release it from the paper. The marker color will bleed through the paper, so choose marker colors that are a close match to the paint colors. This technique imparts a soft, worn look to the transfers, not solid blacks. When choosing your transfer images, select small pictures and remember that they will print in mirror image. The two featured bedstands have six drawers each. If taking on two or more pieces, work on them at the same time, completing each step on each piece.

BEFORE

An unpainted small chest of drawers – not flawed, just bland. Furniture of modest proportions is ideal for busy, interesting treatments.

MATERIALS

- quart (litre) high-adhesion, water-based primer
- quart (litre) eggshell finish latex paint, taupe
- eggshell finish latex paint in three colors, 1 quart (litre) each: pale cinnamon, pale creamy yellow, pale blue-gray
- painting tools: paint brush, small roller, roller tray
- bond paper
- X-acto knife or scissors
- quill pen, calligraphy pen or waterproof marker
- black-and-white photocopied images (make a few extra for testing)
- easy-release painter's tape
- turpentine, or markers in colors similar to the paint (Take a photocopy along when purchasing markers and test the markers. Some new markers do not transfer the images.)
- non-yellowing, water-based varnish
- fine sandpaper (220 grade), tack cloth
- *optional:* can of non-yellowing spray fixative or varnish

1 *Painting the base coat*

Refer to *Painting Basics* (page 34). Prepare and prime the shell and the drawers of the chest.

If working on two chests, as was done in this project, do both chests at once, rather than completing one, then starting on the next.

Paint the body of the chest with two coats of taupe latex paint.

Paint the drawers in pastel colors.

2 *Planning the quotations*

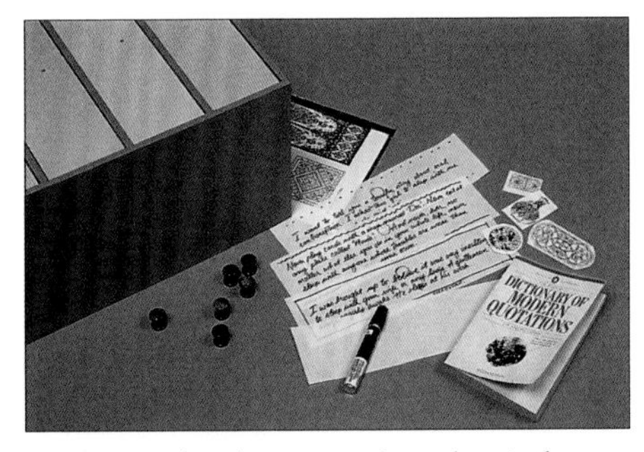

To transcribe the quotations, begin by cutting pieces of paper to fit the drawer fronts. Decide which drawer fronts (all, random drawers or alternating ones) you wish to inscribe. Mark the positions of the hardware onto the paper pieces.

Choose your quotations. Write the quotations on the corresponding pieces of paper, using the quill pen, the calligraphy pen or the marker, to get a sense of placement and how large you can write. Add borders – in zigzags, lazy S's, etc. Place the handwriting pieces and the photocopies in their approximate positions.

3 *Hand writing the quotations*

Line up the drawers, or place them in the chest and tip it onto its back. (Get help if the cabinet is heavy.) Remove a paper piece and copy the quotation onto the drawer front, using the pen or waterproof marker. Avoid the impulse to try writing perfectly. This approach will create hesitant, cramped penmanship. Just let the writing flow smoothly and quickly from the pen. Repeat for all quotations. Allow to dry. Don't throw out the written paper pieces.

Write quotations onto the body of the chest as desired. Allow to dry.

4 *Transferring photocopies*

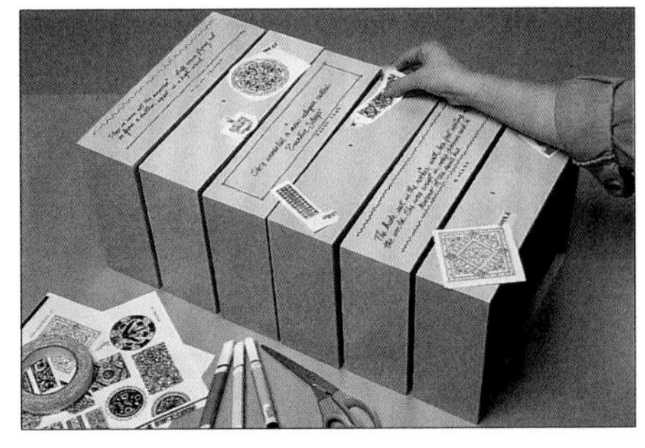

Line up the drawers in order, as they fit into the chest, and position the photocopied images on the drawer fronts. Test the photocopy transfer technique on paper, to get the hang of it, before tackling it on furniture. Don't throw out the paper test pieces.

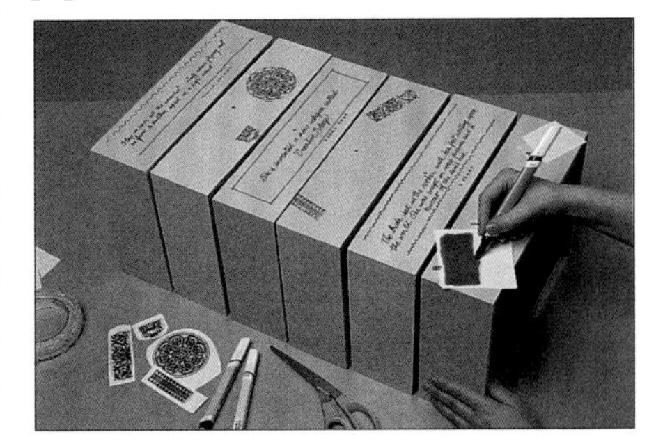

Lay a photocopy face-down onto the drawer front, taping it lightly in place. Cover the back of the image with the marker that matches the paint color. Work quickly, saturating the paper.

If using turpentine, brush it onto the back of the photocopy, saturating the paper.

Pretty Fantastic

Misty Rose Stencils Bedeck A Wooden Table

Step into a pastel-painted Victorian rose garden. This impressionistic paint treatment is nostalgically English country and reminiscent of a turn-of-the-century lady's hatbox, with its hand-painted florals bordered by stripes and sprinkled with tiny blossoms. This adaptable table moves easily into an entryway or a bathroom, kitchen or bedroom.

Read This First

Choose furniture with an English-cottage feeling: simple wooden pieces with some trim, turned legs, or other gentle but not fussy detail. First, the table is painted with a solid base coat of latex paint. If your table has a plastic laminate finish, use melamine paint for the base coat. (See *Melamine Paint,* page 27.) Then flat areas are sponge painted and stenciled with rose and leaf motifs. If pastels are too intense for your color scheme, step 7 shows how to apply a glaze over the paint for a muted look. Or try working in Victorian sepia tones of burgundy, slate blue and taupe. Four different stencils are used in this project, with many being layered. (Patterns are on page 91.) Choose acrylics or the cream paints made for stenciling. Acrylic paints are preferred for their fast drying times. If you use the cream stencil paints available in craft stores, expect each color to take several days to dry.

MATERIALS

- quart (litre) high-adhesion, water-based primer (or spray primer)
- quart (litre) eggshell finish latex paint, powder blue
- painting tools: paint brush, small roller, roller tray
- synthetic or natural sponge for sponge painting
- for sponging: latex and/or acrylic paints – pastel pink, pastel blue-green, off-white
- stencil plastic (available at art supply and craft stores (or lightweight cardboard))
- scissors or X-acto knife
- pink colored pencil
- for stenciling: tubes of acrylics (and an inexpensive square-tipped artist's brush), or cream stencil paints (and a stencil brush) – acid green, pastel blue-green, pastel pink, medium pink
- for hand painting: tubes of acrylics – yellow, off-white, deep blue, medium green, dark blue-gray
- fine-point artist's brush and medium-sized artist's brush
- easy-release painter's tape or masking tape
- quart (litre) non-yellowing, water-based varnish
- *optional:* spray glue; scrap paper, dropsheets

BEFORE

A pleasantly proportioned 1940s wooden table with turned spindle legs and gingerbread trim. When the flaking varnish is scraped down and the legs and trim are repaired, it becomes the perfect foil for a Victorian treatment.

1 *Painting*

Refer to *Painting Basics* (page 34). Prepare, prime and paint the table with two coats of powder blue paint.

Allow to dry. If you wish to antique the table, do not prime it.

2 *Sponge painting*

Mix each of the colors listed for sponging.

Use easy-release painter's tape or masking tape to mask off the area to be sponge painted.

Mix the pastel pink paint with water to a soupy consistency, or add glaze. (See *Glaze,* page 28.) Tear off a chunk of sponge and dampen it slightly with water. Then saturate it with paint. Squeeze out most of the paint.

Using a pouncing motion, sponge the tabletop (and any other sections that you wish), leaving about half the blue showing through. Make the coverage in some spots heavier, to resemble cloud formations. The base coat (powder blue) will begin disappearing, with each subsequent sponged-on color gaining prominence.

3 *Sponge painting, continued*

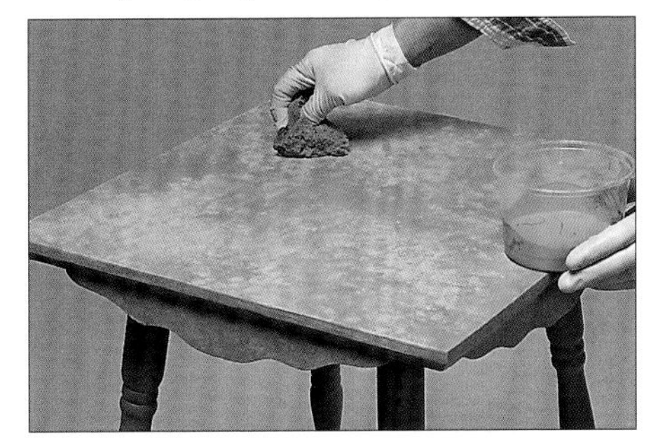

While the pink paint is still damp, sponge paint over it with pastel blue-green, allowing both pink and blue to show through.

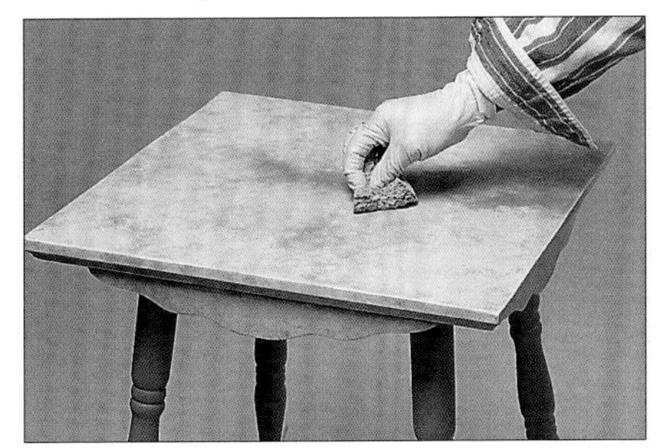

Sponge paint a final coat of off-white, allowing the previous colors to glow through. Allow to dry.

4 *Preparing stencils*

While the sponge painting is drying, trace the rose and leaf patterns onto the stencil plastic (or similar material) and cut out the center shaded areas. The cutting can be done with scissors or an X-acto knife.

For easier stenciling, spray-glue the backs of the stencils. Let the glue dry at least an hour to a light tackiness. (If the glue is too sticky, it will lift the background paint.)

Try a few test stencils on paper before stenciling the table. Press the stencil onto paper and, using an artist's paint brush or a stencil brush (a round brush with stiff bristles and a flat end), paint the center of the stencil. A paint brush will give a hand-painted look with brushstrokes, while the stencil brush will give smooth color. Add freehand lines or details.

5 *Stenciling*

Using the *Rose in Bloom* stencil and a pink colored pencil, mark the positions of roses on the table. Set this stencil aside.

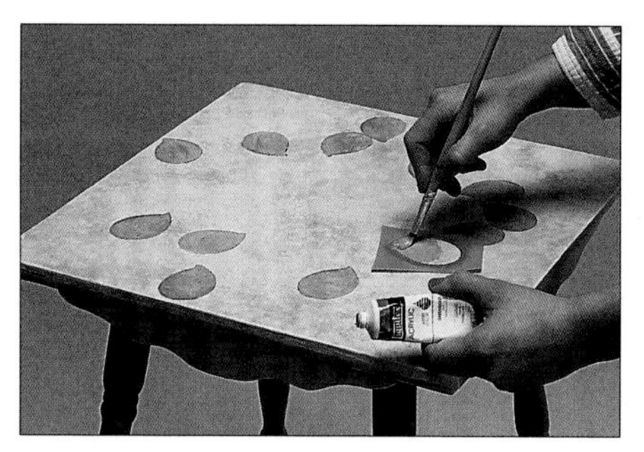

Using the *Large Leaf* stencil and acid green paint, stencil leaves around and overlapping the marked roses. Lay the stencil onto the surface, gently pressing it down for adhesion. Then paint the full opening to all edges. Carefully lift the stencil while the paint is still wet, and proceed to the next leaf. Be careful not to lay the stencil over wet paint. It's advisable first to stencil in corners of the table, adding more leaves in between as the paint dries.

Using the *Small Leaf* stencil and the pastel blue-green paint, stencil leaves adjoining the large leaves. Allow them to overlap the large leaves in some places, and in other places stop at the outline of the large leaves.

Using the *Rose in Bloom* stencil and pastel pink, stencil the roses where you marked them, covering parts of some leaves and painting around others.

Using the *Center Rose* stencil and the medium-pink paint, stencil centers on top of the roses. The centers can be stenciled on the roses in any direction. There is no particular way they must be lined up.

6 *Hand painting*

Mix a small amount of yellow into some off-white paint. Using a medium-sized artist's brush, paint random highlights onto the roses.

Paint short, curved outline strokes in and around the roses, using the deep-blue paint and a fine-point artist's brush. Paint random shadows and center lines onto the leaves, using a medium green and a fine-point artist's brush.

Create clusters of small dots in among the roses, using the dark-blue-gray paint and a fine-point artist's brush.

Paint the spindles on the legs, or add other details such as stripes, as shown here, with colors of your choice.

7 *Varnishing and glazing*

Enrich color and protect the paint by varnishing with non-yellowing, water-based varnish. If the colors are stronger than desired, glaze them to reduce their intensity by adding a very small amount of off-white paint to the varnish, mixing thoroughly. Brush onto the table as you would with pure varnish. (See *Varnishing,* page 48.)

STENCIL PATTERNS

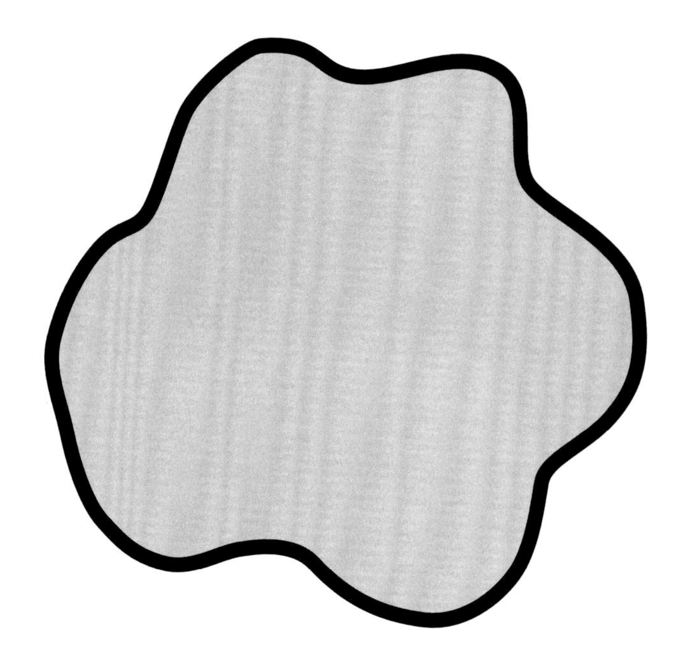

Rose in Bloom

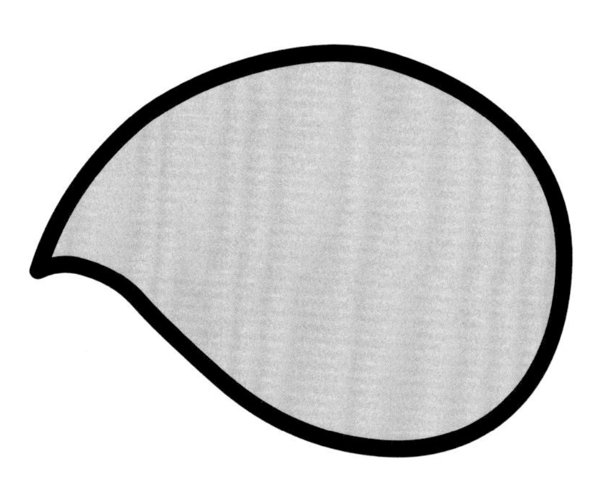

Large Leaf

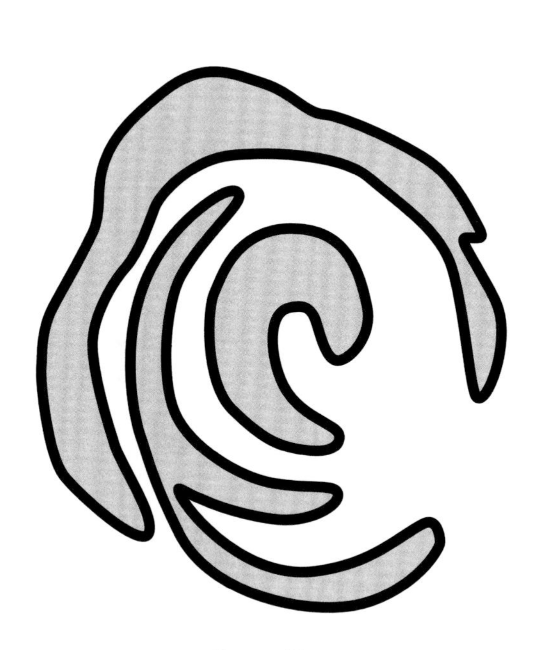

Center Rose

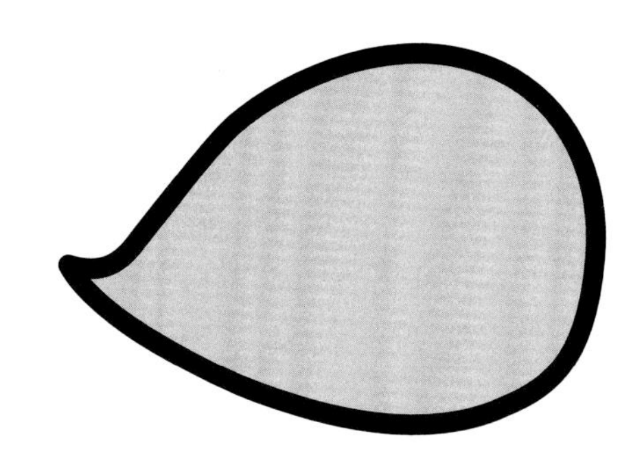

Small Leaf

Sheer Delight

GAUZY, PRINTED FLORAL VINES ENTWINE OVER PAINTED TRELLIS

Muted glazes layer pink springtime roses, purple and blue morning glories, and dusty-green foliage. These block-printed floral vines trail and weave their way through lattice over a subdued, neutral ground. Create a fresh and lovely painterly garden for a sunny solarium or a foyer, bedroom, bathroom or dressing room. This is a very modern approach to romance.

5 *Spray painting lattice*

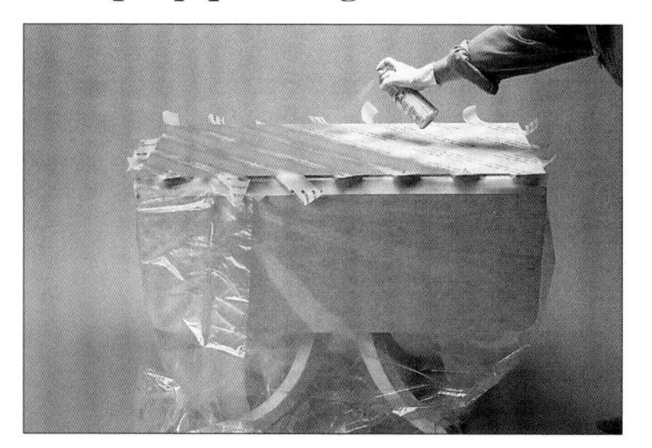

Spray paint the tabletop with one or two coats, following the manufacturer's directions. (See *Spray Painting,* page 44.) Remove the tape strips when the paint is dry to the touch. Allow to dry thoroughly.

Repeat steps 3, 4 and 5, starting at the same end of the table but this time laying the tape in the opposite direction, across the spray-painted lines. Apply the spray paint. Allow to dry.

6 *Shadows*

Optional: To give the lattice depth, mix a small quantity of medium-gray paint, either acrylic or latex. Using a fine-point artist's brush, paint shadows on one side of the lattice lines where they cross other lines.

7 *Drawing vines*

Raise the table leaves into the up position. Using the pencil crayon or chalk, lightly sketch the direction of branches and vines for roses on one table leaf, and for morning glories on the other table leaf. The vines should begin at opposite corners of the table and follow a curvy S shape, then bend around and overlap on the lattice. Draw generous curves to accommodate the leaves and floral patterns. Add branches to fill space.

8 *Cutting block prints*

Transfer the patterns (pages 98 and 99), including tabs, by tracing or photocopying them. Trace the patterns onto the foam. Cut out the foam block-print shapes with scissors or an X-acto knife.

Using an X-acto knife, score along the lines inside the blocks. Try not to cut right through the foam. The scored lines will print darker, giving detail to the print.

9 *Printing*

Do some test prints on paper. Using a medium-sized, square-tipped artist's brush, paint glaze onto the surface of the foam block. Press the block face-down and apply even pressure over the surface. Lift off by pulling gently on the tab. Try using one color. Then try painting patches of several shades of one color on a single block. The block can be used several times with one load of glaze, producing interesting variations in the intensity of the print.

With the table leaves in the up position, begin printing the morning glory leaves in a variety of greens on one table leaf and onto the lattice, following the chalk lines for the vines. Overlapping the morning glory leaves gives wonderful depth to the pattern. Allow room for blossoms.

Continue, printing the rose leaves. Wash out the blocks and set them aside.

Add blossoms and buds, with morning glories in shades of blue and purple and with roses in shades of pink, red and/or orange. When the floral prints are complete, add the *Sepal Leaf Cluster* print at the base of the rose and morning glory blossoms.

10 *Freehand painting*

Using a fine-point artist's brush and glaze or acrylic paint, paint the vines and branches in a green/brown tone. (Mix green with some pink or purple to get green/brown.) Load the brush with thinned paint, and paint in a long sweeping motion. Do not worry about painting directly onto the lines. Use the lines only as a guide.

Add more leaves or blossoms where desired.

11 *Varnishing and finishing*

Enrich color and protect the paint job by varnishing with two or three coats of non-yellowing, water-based varnish. Sand lightly with fine sandpaper and wipe with a tack cloth between each coat. When varnish is dry, use an X-acto knife to cut along the crease where the table leaves meet the table. Lightly sand any excess varnish with fine sandpaper. If sanding clouds the varnish, touch up these areas with another coat. (See *Varnishing,* page 48.)

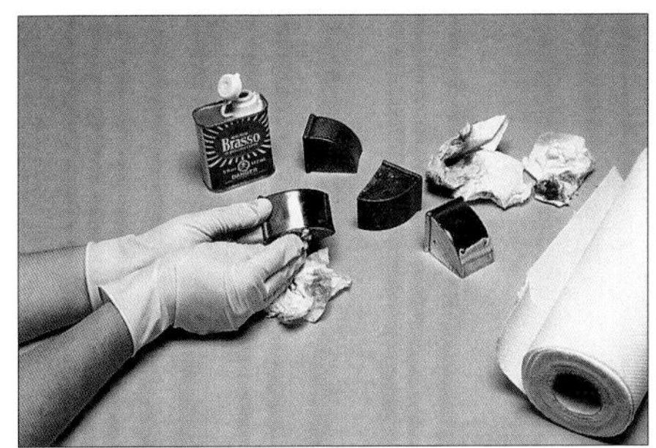

Polish brass feet or other hardware, and attach the hardware.

Patterns for Foam Block Prints

Rose, Full Bloom

Rose, Profile Bloom

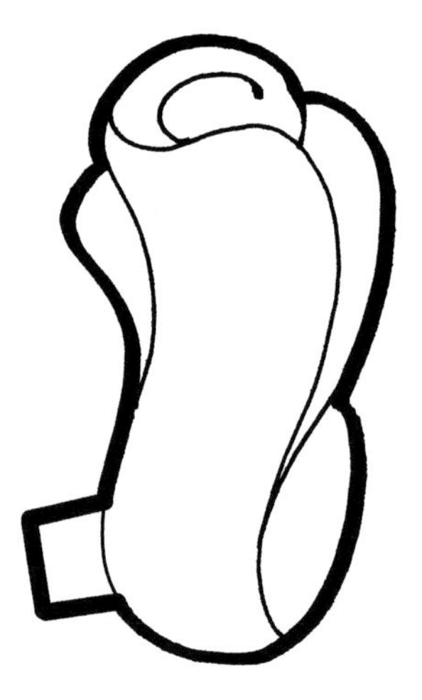

Rosebud

Rose Leaf

Sepal Leaf Cluster

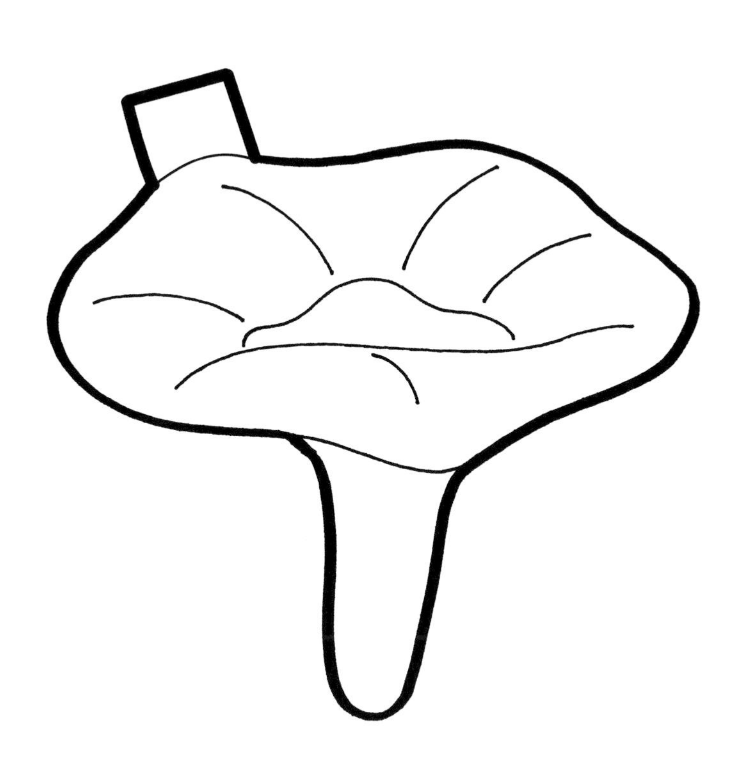

Morning Glory, Profile Bloom

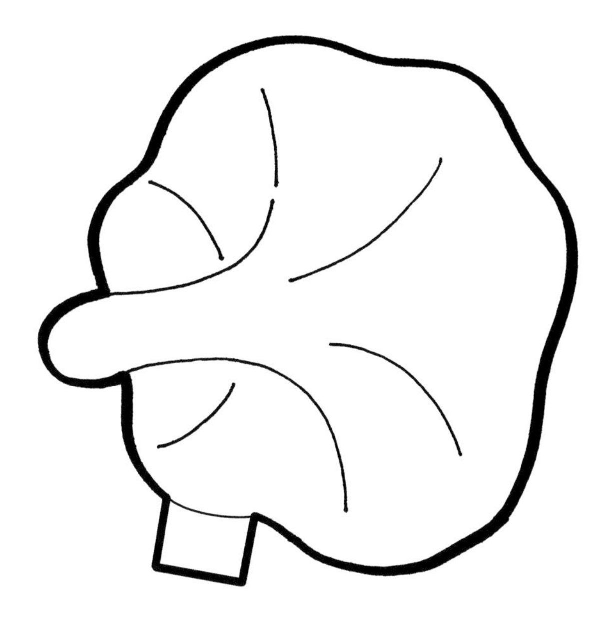

Morning Glory Bloom

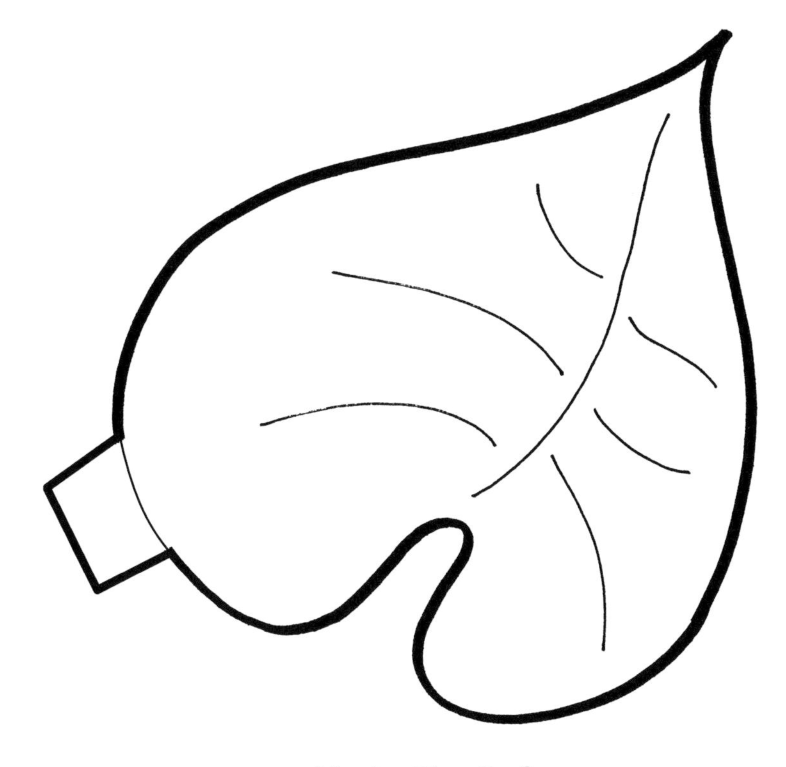

Morning Glory Leaf

Morning Glory Leaf

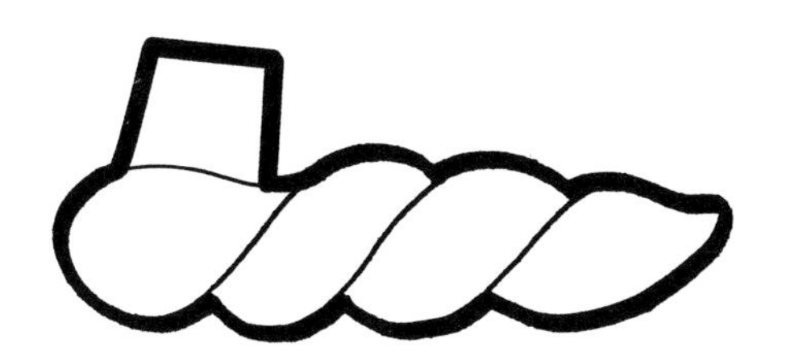

Morning Glory Bud

Full Cry through the Homestead

Times Tables

Simple Stenciling Creates A Timely Classic

Whatever the dimensions – from a lamp table to a full dining table – any round table is suited to a traditional clock face composition. The neutral tones and traditional Roman numeral clock face make this table treatment an instant classic that fits virtually any room. This project is completed in three simple stages. The difficult part is deciding what time to set the clock's hands at, in perpetuity.

Read This First

After the base of the table is painted with a black base coat, three easy treatments complete the clock face – sponge painting, stenciling and some hand painting. If your table has a plastic laminate finish, use melamine paint for the base coat. (See *Melamine Paint,* page 27.) The sponge painting is very quick, giving the clock face an antiqued, parchmentlike appearance. Then Roman numerals are stenciled in black. Patterns for the stencils – a I, an X, a V, and a clock hand – are on page 105. The three numerals are all that are required because they will be sized and combined as needed. The paint with the fastest drying time for stenciling is acrylic paint. Cream paints, sold in craft stores, are the stencil paints with the consistency of shoe polish. If you choose them, remember that most require several days to dry. Spray paint can be used, but the overspray is a problem, requiring extensive masking for each numeral. This is a weekend project that renders impressive results for the time invested.

MATERIALS

- pint (.5 litre) eggshell finish latex paint, off-white
- paint brush, 1½ in. (4 cm) wide
- paper and easy-release painter's tape, for masking
- can of acrylic spray paint, black
- waterproof marker, black
- fine-point artist's brush
- sponge for sponge painting
- small quantity latex or acrylic paint, taupe
- chalk or pencil
- ruler and set-square or other right angle
- beam compass; or string, hammer and small nail
- stencil plastic (available at art supply and craft stores) or lightweight cardboard
- access to photocopier
- utility or X-acto knife
- tube of acrylic paint and square-tipped artist's brush, or cream paint and a stencil brush
- quart (litre) non-yellowing, water-based varnish
- *optional:* spray glue; scrap paper or dropsheet
- *optional:* small quantity black touch-up paint
- *optional:* large, flat brass button with a shank-back; power drill; white carpenter's glue
- *optional:* small quantity medium-gray acrylic paint

BEFORE

At first glance, a two-tiered table. In reality, a pleasing oak base with a mismatched top.

1 *Painting the base coat*

If possible, remove the top from the base of the table. (Recruit help if the table is large or heavy.) The top tier of this table was discarded because it was warped beyond repair.

Paint the tabletop with two coats of off-white latex paint. Allow to dry.

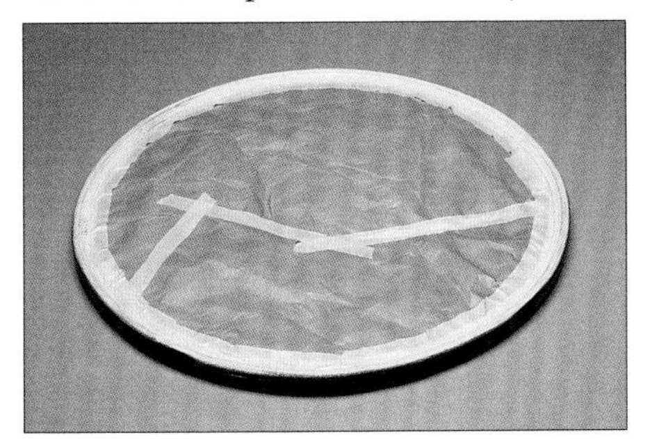

Mask the top of the table with paper and tape around the edge, inside the lip (if the table has one); or leave a 1 in. (2.5 cm) border. Turn the table over and, with the black spray paint, paint the underside of the tabletop. (See *Spray Painting,* page 44.) Allow to dry.

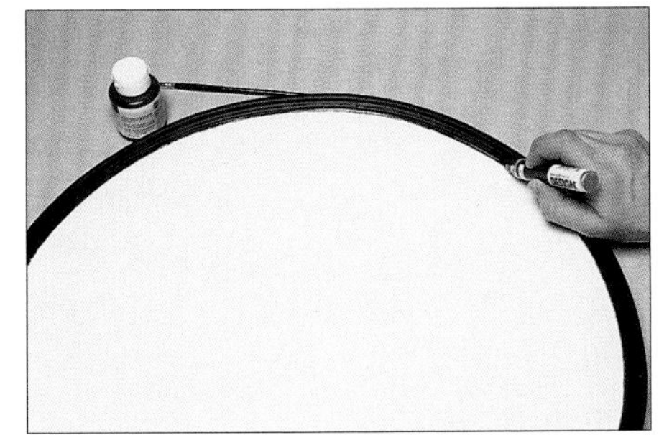

Turn the tabletop right-side-up and spray paint to the masked edge. Remove the masking. If the line of paint is wavy or uneven, draw a smooth line with a waterproof marker and fill in the gaps with a fine-point artist's brush and black paint.

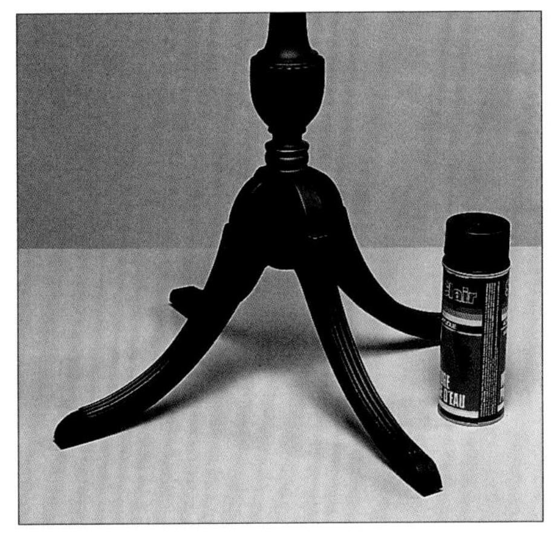

Spray paint the base black. Apply as many coats as needed for dense coverage. Allow to dry.

2 *Sponge painting*

Give the background of the clock face the look of parchment by sponge painting it with taupe paint. If desired, tape the edges to prevent sponging onto the black rim.

Thin the taupe paint with water to a liquid consistency, or add glaze. (See *Glaze,* page 28.) Tear off a chunk of sponge and dampen it slightly with water. It should be only slightly moist. Saturate the sponge with taupe paint and squeeze out excess. Using a patting motion, sponge the taupe paint over the off-white background, allowing about half the background color to show through. Avoid getting paint on the black edge. Remove tape and allow paint to dry. Make any needed touch-ups required.

3 *Planning the clock face*

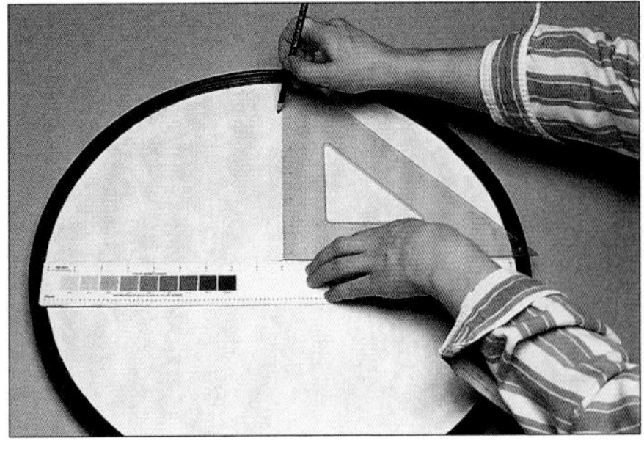

Measure the center of the table and mark lightly with chalk or pencil. Divide and mark the table into quarters by laying a ruler across the center of the table, marking the halves. Then, using a set-square or other right angle, mark the top and bottom quarters.

Using a beam compass and a waterproof black marker, draw a line about 1 in. (2.5 cm) inside the edge of the circle.

A beam compass will give the best results, but if you don't own one try this low-tech method. Drive a small nail halfway into the center of the table. Tie string to the nail at one end and to a waterproof black marker at the other, at a correct distance to draw the circle. Holding the marker straight up, and maintaining tension on the string, draw the circle, carefully connecting the ends.

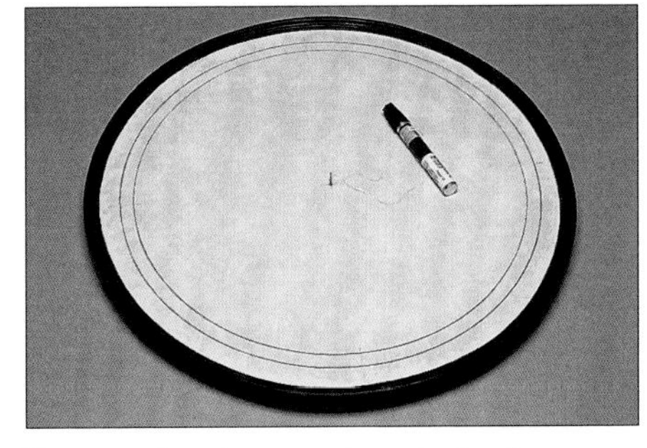

Repeat, drawing another circle about ¾ in. (2 cm) inside the first circle.

4 *Stenciling*

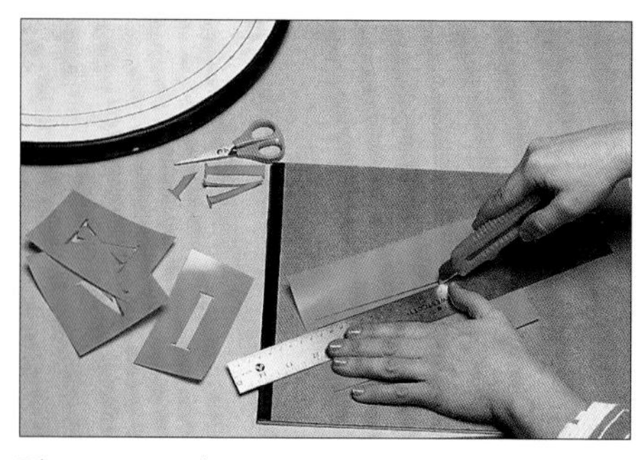

Photocopy the patterns (page 105) to the appropriate size, and trace them onto stencil plastic or lightweight cardboard. Cut them out, using a utility or an X-acto knife (sharp new blade, please).

Stenciling is easier and the results are cleaner if the backs of the stencils are sprayed with spray glue and allowed to dry for at least one hour, until lightly tacky. If the glue is too sticky, it will pull off background paint.

Mark the positions of numerals by measuring and dividing each quarter of the clock into thirds. Mark these divisions with pencil. Not all clocks have all twelve numerals. If you prefer, stencil only the XII, the III, the VI and the IX and use small decorative designs for the other hours.

Position a stencil with the top of the numeral on the curved line. (Numerals read right-side-up from the center of the clock face.)

When stenciling, try to visualize the full numeral and work to center the numeral at the mark. For example, with the III, the center I would be at the mark, with the remaining I's on either side. Press the stencil in place, making a light bond. Using black paint – acrylic and a square-tipped artist's brush, or cream stencil paint and a stencil brush (a round brush with stiff bristles and a flat end) – fill in the stencil. Remove the stencil. Stencil the numerals in random order to avoid smearing wet paint.

Stencil the clock hands, starting at the center. Make sure to stencil the minute hand longer than the hour hand. Allow to dry.

5 *Decorative details*

Optional: In the centre of the table, drill a large, shallow hole for the shank-back of a large brass button. Press the shank into the hole, gluing the button in place with carpenter's glue. The brass button will cover the center of the clock where the hands join.

Optional: Using a fine-point artist's brush and black paint, add decorative triangles, floral motifs, diamonds or other motifs to the clock face.

Using a fine-point artist's brush and medium-gray paint, paint a narrow shadow along the bottom edges of the clock hands, giving them a three-dimensional appearance.

6 *Varnishing*

Protect the paint and enrich color on the clock face by applying non-yellowing, water-based varnish. (See *Varnishing,* page 48.)

Reattach the top to the rest of the table.

I X V

Clock Numeral and Clock Hand Stencil Patterns

Make the clock hand as long as necessary for your clock face.

Art in Craft

Stenciled Copper Leaf Offsets Layered Color and Crafted Copper

Acid green, layered over brilliant blue paint and spiced with crafted and stenciled copper, renders an outdated desk a vibrant piece of contemporary art. This desk has aggressive texture, color and pattern – elements that create a novel, fast-forward piece. Not for the faint of heart, this combination of tactile materials, random stencils and vivid colors takes some nerve. But accolades from admirers will reward your daring decision.

Read This First

Acid and cool colors rub up against each other in this paint technique. The paint treatment consists of layering color, then lightly sanding the coats with a hard plastic stripping sponge to expose the underlying colors. If your desk has a plastic laminate finish, use melamine paint for the base coat. (See *Melamine Paint,* page 27.) Also demonstrated is dry brushing, a technique with an effect similar to sanded paint. The stenciling can be done in any contrasting color or in a metallic leaf – gold, copper or silver – with a purchased or homemade stencil. For metallic leaf, you'll need the compatible leaf, adhesive which is fairly thick in consistency, not the watery variety, and sealer. For the copper cut-outs buy one or more sheets of copper, the type used for copper-burnishing kits. You will also need copper etching fluid and patina in blue or green. These chemical treatments, used to oxidize the copper and produce a patina, are available at art supply and craft stores.

MATERIALS

- quart (litre) high-adhesion, water-based primer
- eggshell finish latex paint, 1 quart (litre) each: brilliant blue, moss green, chartreuse green
- painting tools: paint brush, small roller, roller tray
- plastic paint-stripping sponge
- rag or scrap paper
- inexpensive square-tipped artist's brush, ½ in. (1.25 cm) wide
- purchased stencil, or stencil plastic or cardboard (step 4)
- spray glue; scrap paper or dropsheet
- copper leaf and compatible adhesive (use a thick, not a watery, adhesive) and sealer
- sheet of thin copper, heavy scissors
- etching fluid for copper (often called "Metal Master," and available at art supply and craft stores)
- rag or paint brush
- patina blue or green fluid (available at art supply and craft stores), soft paint brush
- sealer (made by manufacturer of the patina)
- small hammer and small brass nails
- quart (litre) non-yellowing, water-based varnish
- *optional:* needle-nosed pliers

BEFORE

Lacking personality, this mediocre desk deserves some zip.

1 *Painting*

Refer to *Painting Basics* (page 34). Prepare, prime and paint the body of the desk with two coats of brilliant blue latex paint. Paint the drawer fronts with two coats of moss green. Allow to dry.

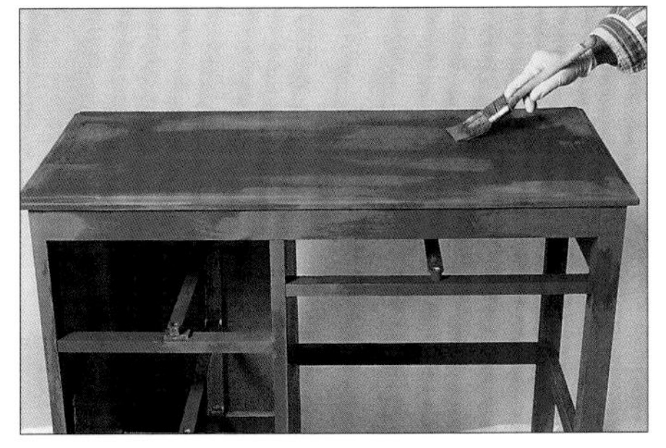

Paint moss green over the body of the desk, brushing it on at random. Allow to dry.

Paint chartreuse in random areas over the drawer fronts. Allow to dry.

2 *Painting and distressing*

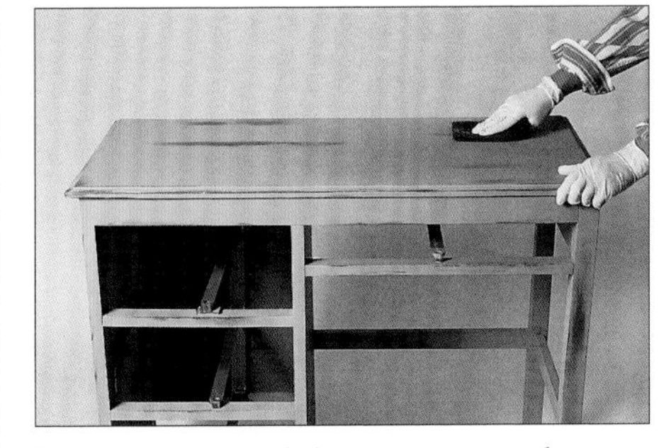

Paint one coat of chartreuse over the body of the desk, with as much coverage as possible. When the paint is dry to the touch, firmly buff it with the paint-stripping sponge, removing layers of paint and exposing the undercoats in areas where the desk would naturally show wear, such as along all trim, on corners and in random spots on the top and sides. Try not to rub through all layers to the primer. If you accidentally do, however, you can touch up areas later.

Paint the drawer fronts with the brilliant blue. Buff through the paint, exposing various layers.

3 *Dry-brush technique*

Using a dry-brush technique add more contrasting color to the surface, if desired. Dip the artist's brush into the paint. Wipe excess paint onto a rag or piece of scrap paper. Brush the remaining paint onto the desk surface. This is a lot like wiping out a used brush, leaving a thin, somewhat transparent layer of paint on the surface. The paint will be dense where you start, becoming thinner the more you brush. Make any touch-ups as required.

4 *Stenciling copper leaf*

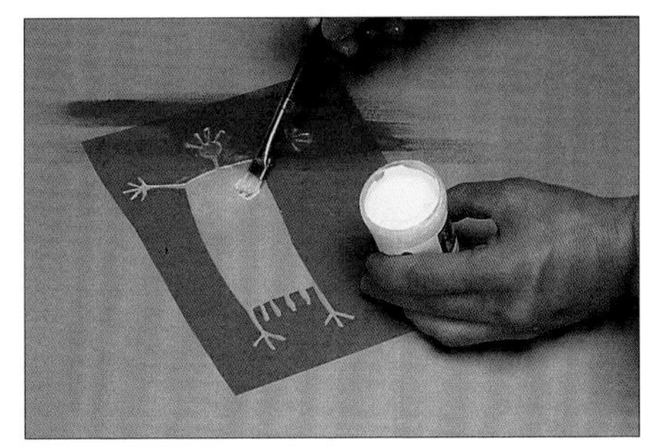

Add stenciled copper leaf designs onto the desk in a random fashion. Use a purchased stencil, or cut a design from stencil plastic (available at craft stores) or lightweight cardboard. For ease of stenciling, coat the back of the stencil with spray glue. Allow the stencil to sit for an hour or more until the glue is lightly tacky. Lay the stencil onto the desk and paint the image area with adhesive for the copper leaf. Remove the stencil. Repeat in all locations where a stenciled pattern is desired. Allow the adhesive to set. It will remain very tacky.

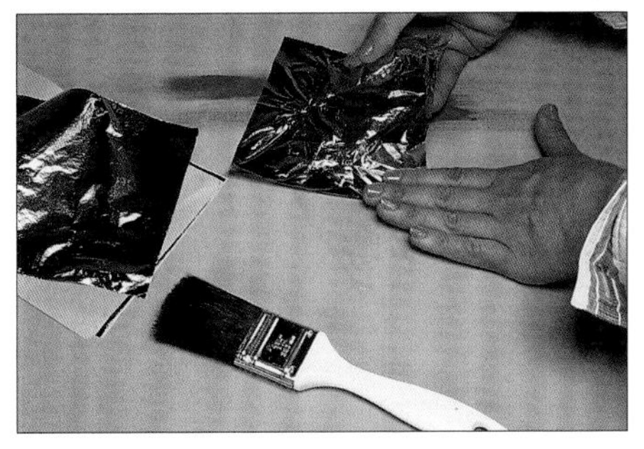

Lay a sheet of copper leaf onto the adhesive. Burnish it with your fingers.

Using a small paint brush, brush excess copper leaf from the edges of the image. Repeat for all stenciled areas of adhesive. Using the sealer for the copper leaf, paint the stenciled copper leaf designs.

5 *Sheet copper*

Draw patterns and trace them, or cut shapes freehand from the sheet copper. *When cutting this copper, be extremely careful.* The edges can be very sharp. Injuries are more painful and annoying than paper cuts. (Wearing a cast-off pair of leather gloves can help protect you.)

Lay the cut-outs right-side-up on paper and paint them with etching fluid.

Using a rag or a paint brush, coat the cut-outs with either patina blue or green. Allow to dry and to turn color. Check the instructions on the jar of sealer to determine the length of time you need to wait before sealing (often three days).

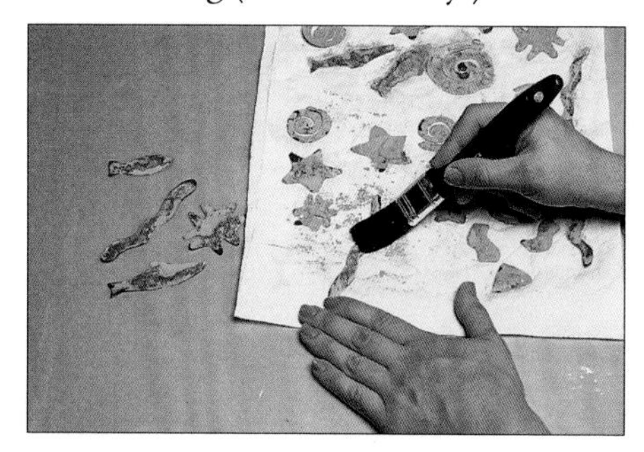

Using a dry soft paint brush, brush away excess patina.

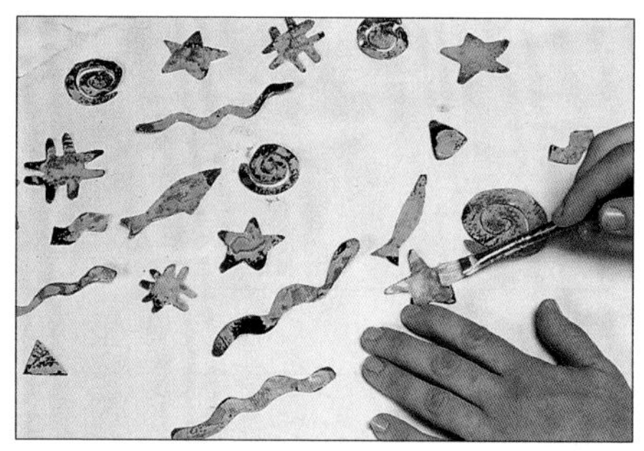

Coat the patina side of the copper with sealer. Allow to dry.

Using a small hammer and small brass nails, nail the copper cut-outs in place on the desk. If the nails are very short, use needle-nosed pliers to hold the nails while hammering.

Protect the paint, smooth the edges of the copper pieces and enrich color by painting the desk with two or three coats of non-yellowing, water-based varnish. (See *Varnishing,* page 48.)

Attach the hardware.

Using specialty treatments such as metallics on a textured ground is what makes the difference between painter and artist. Shown here, reverse-stenciling on a sponge-painted background. (See Vanity Flair, page 68.)

Seating

Sitting Pretty With Professionally Crafted Cushions And Seats

The seat of a chair is more than a place to park. Chair seats and cushions offer a design opportunity to add texture, color and pattern with fabric – along with a higher degree of comfort. Try to find an upholstery supplier that sells upholsterer's-quality high-density foam, batting, and dust-cover cloth. Dust-cover cloth is the non-fraying fabric that goes under the seat to cover raw edges and bare plywood. If you can, take along the plywood base from the old cushion as a pattern, and have the foam pieces cut to fit.

Following are instructions for a basic seat cushion, a piped seat cushion, and a woven webbing seat, along with two treatments for backrest cushions – tailored and shirred. Only the piped cushion requires sewing.

Above, *the chair on the left has a basic seat cushion and a shirred backrest cushion. The chair on the right has a piped seat cushion.* ***Left,*** *both chairs have basic seat cushions and tailored backrest cushions.*

Basic Seat Cushion

Read This First

This seat cushion is the type that looks like a large soft cookie. Use this treatment primarily on round chair seats. Square seats tend to look better with a straight-sided or piped cushion. Choose the thickness of the foam, between one and two inches (2.5 to 5 cm), depending on the style of the chair. If the thicker foam will obscure detailing or be ungainly in height, choose a thinner foam. It will look better, but the trade-off will be a harder chair and slightly less comfort for those sitting on it. Buy plywood that is good one side. This means that one side has a smooth finish, while the other is knotty and rough. The good side of the plywood will be positioned down on the seat. (Good both sides, which is much more expensive, is not necessary.)

MATERIALS

- plywood, ½ in. (1.25 cm) thick, good one side, cut to fit the seat of the chair
- high-density upholstery foam, 1 to 2 in (2.5 to 5 cm) thick, cut to fit plywood
- fabric, 8 in. (20 cm) larger than the plywood both in length and in width
- iron
- ruler and marker
- scissors
- batting, 6 in. (15 cm) larger than the plywood both in length and in width
- stapler and ⅜ in. (1 cm) staples
- non-fraying upholstery dust-cover cloth (enough to cover the plywood)
- screws (to reattach cushion to chair), screwdriver
- *optional:* jigsaw
- *optional:* spray glue; scrap paper or dropsheet
- *optional:* lining (step 5)

1 *Getting started*

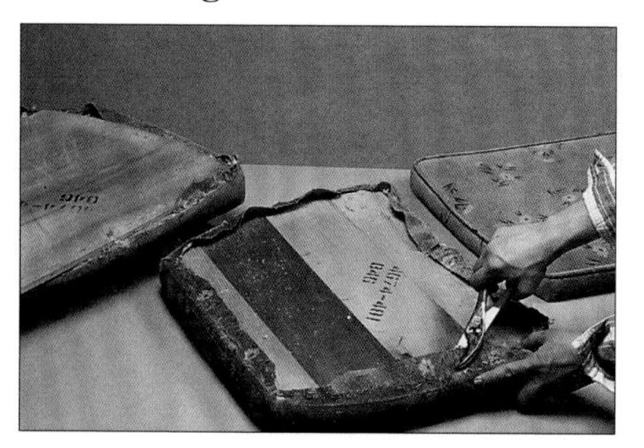

Remove the fabric and foam from the underlying plywood. Clean the plywood as thoroughly as possible, removing any mold and staples.

If the old plywood is beyond salvation, have a new piece cut or cut one yourself with a jigsaw. The new plywood should be ½ in. (1.25 cm) thick, good one side.

Have a piece of high-density upholstery foam cut to match the size and shape of the plywood.

2 *Cutting fabric*

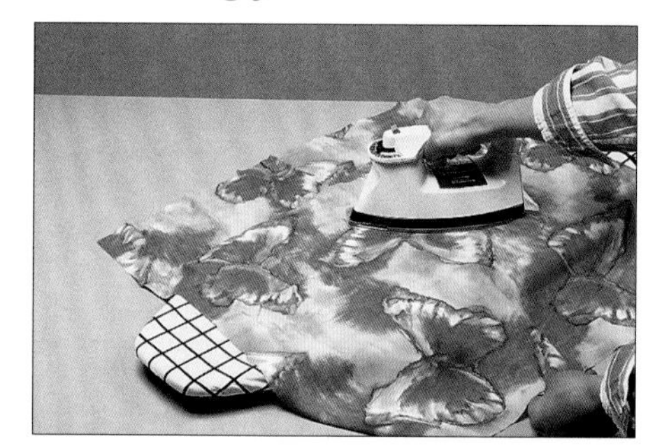

Iron the fabric.

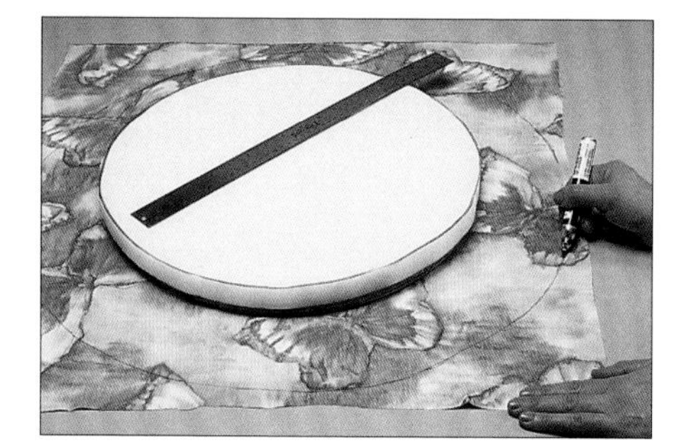

Lay the foam or the plywood onto the wrong side of the fabric. Measure and mark the fabric 4 in. (10 cm) from the edge of the foam. Do this at regular intervals around the perimeter of the foam. Join the marks to make a continuous solid line.

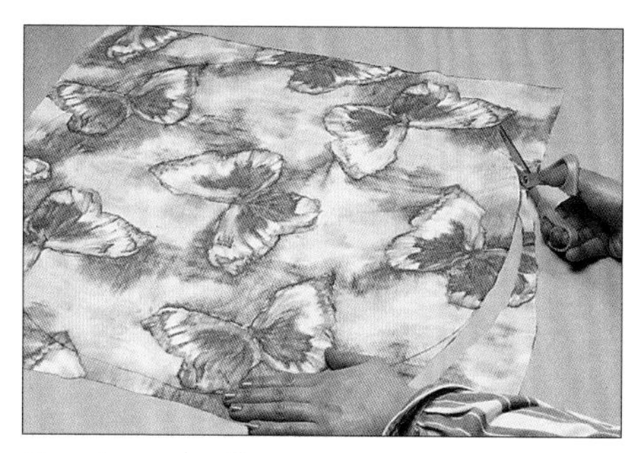

Cut along the line.

3 *Laminating foam to plywood*

Optional: Gluing the foam to the plywood can reduce slippage. Lay down some scrap paper or a dropsheet and place the foam onto it. Check the directions on the spray-glue label for making a permanent bond. Spray the foam with glue.

Lay the rough side of the plywood on the gluey foam, centering it.

4 *Batting*

Lay the plywood/foam onto the batting. Lift the batting up, against the side of the foam, marking the batting at the top edge of the foam. Do this all the around the foam.

Cut the batting along the marked line.

Optional: With the plywood/foam centered on the circle of batting, foam-side-down, spray-glue a section of the overhanging batting. Fold the glued section up onto the foam. Repeat until the batting is glued to the perimeter of the foam.

5 *Stapling*

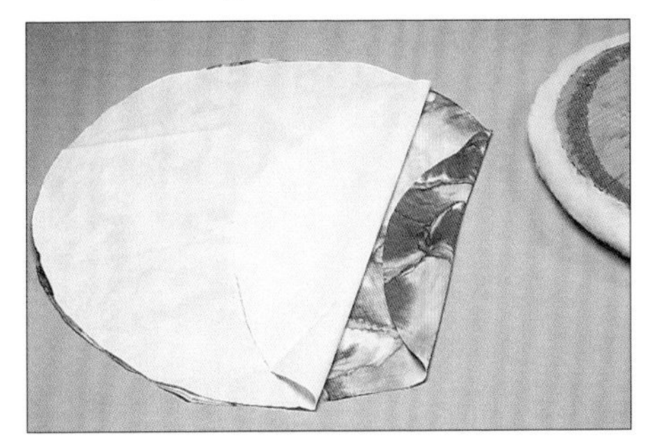

If the cushion fabric is lightweight, cut a lining from a woven material such as broadcloth. Lay the fabric face-down, with the lining on top.

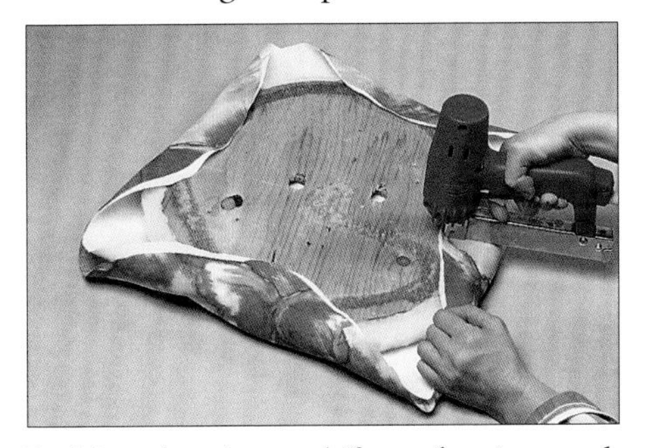

Position the plywood/foam/batting sandwich, batting-side-down, onto the center of the fabric. Gently but firmly, pull and staple the fabric to the plywood in four places, equal distances apart.

Gently but firmly, pull and staple the fabric to the plywood between each of the four staples, keeping the pressure even.

Gently but firmly, pull and staple the fabric to the plywood between each of the eight staples, keeping the pressure even.

Gently but firmly, pull and staple the fabric to the plywood between the staples. Continue until the fabric is stapled evenly all around.

6 *Finishing*

Cut a circle of dust-cover cloth slightly larger than the circle of staples, but smaller than the bottom of the cushion. Staple it to the bottom of the cushion, starting with four equidistant staples. Then staple between them, as you did to staple the cushion fabric, until the full perimeter is stapled.

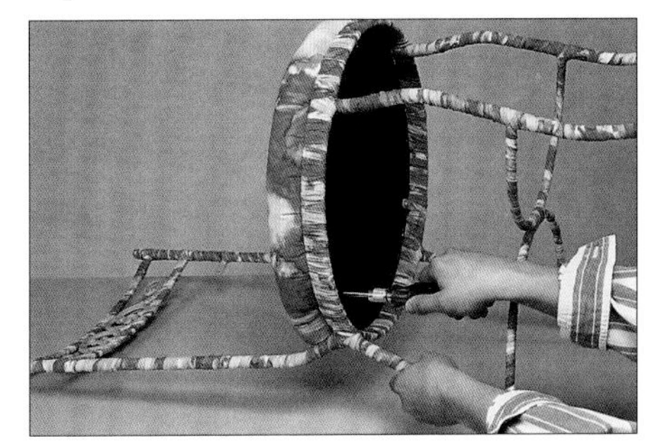

Reattach the cushion to the chair by screwing appropriately sized screws into the seat frame and the plywood of the cushion. Work from underneath the seat.

Piped Seat Cushion

Read This First

Making a piped seat cushion takes some planning and sewing ability, although the sewing is actually basic and straightforward. The piping gives the cushion an elegant, crisp finish. Piping is available in braids or wovens, and it comes in a wide range of colors, prints and finishes, from shiny to matte. Choose a piping that will coordinate with the fabric, yet stand out enough to accentuate the tailored edge. If you have never sewn piping with a piping foot on your sewing machine, here's a chance to try it and see how professional the results are. The sewing goes faster and is easier if a piping foot is used. It keeps the piping on track and the sewing uniform. If a piping foot is not available, use a zipper foot.

Materials

- plywood, ½ in. (1.25 cm) thick, good one side, cut to fit the seat of the chair
- high-density upholstery foam, 2 in. (5 cm) thick, cut to match the plywood
- paper, pencil, ruler
- fabric, approx. ½ yd. (.5 m) for each cushion
- scissors
- piping (measure perimeter of cushion and add 6 in. (15 cm))
- dressmaker's pins
- sewing machine with piping foot
- thread to match fabric
- batting, 6 in. (15 cm) larger than the plywood both in length and in width
- stapler and ⅜ in. (1 cm) staples
- non-fraying upholstery dust-cover cloth (enough to cover the plywood)
- screws (to reattach cushion to chair), screwdriver
- *optional:* jigsaw
- *optional:* zipper foot
- *optional:* spray glue; scrap paper or drop-sheet

1 *Getting started*

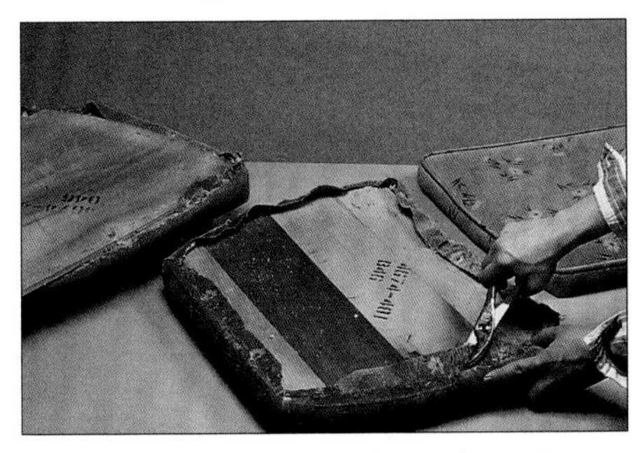

Remove the fabric and foam from the underlying plywood. Clean the plywood as thoroughly as possible, removing any mold and staples.

If the old plywood is beyond repair, have a new piece cut or cut one yourself with a jigsaw. The new plywood should be ½ in. (1.25 cm) thick, good one side.

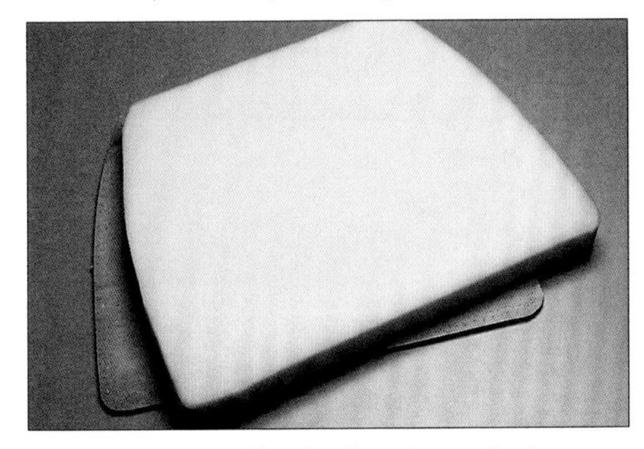

Have a piece of high-density upholstery foam, 2 in. (5 cm) thick, professionally cut to match the size and shape of the plywood.

2 *Drafting a pattern*

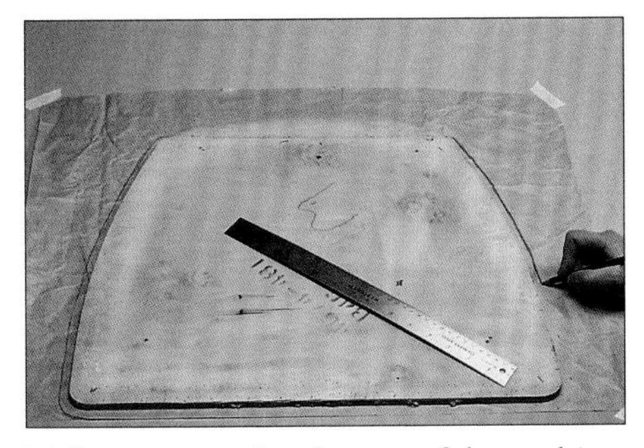

Make a pattern for the top of the cushion cover. Lay the plywood onto paper and trace closely around it. Using a ruler, measure and mark a ½ in. (1.25 cm) seam allowance from the plywood edge all around the perimeter. Then join the marks to create a cutting line.

3 *Cutting fabric*

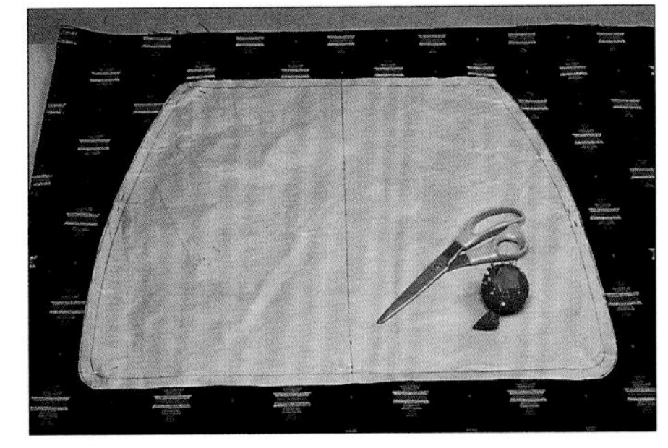

Cut out the pattern and lay it onto the fabric, centering it carefully onto the fabric's design. If the design printed on the fabric is directional (vines climbing a trellis, for example), it should run from the front of the cushion "up" to the back.

On fabric with a geometric pattern, the placement should match for all cushions. Pin the pattern in place and cut out the fabric for all cushions.

For the sides of the cushion cover, cut strips of fabric, 6 in. (15 cm) wide, across the width of the fabric. Cut the strips to match up with the fabric design of the cushion tops, taking into consideration the width of seam allowances. Usually, one width of fabric will circle one cushion.

4 *Sewing*

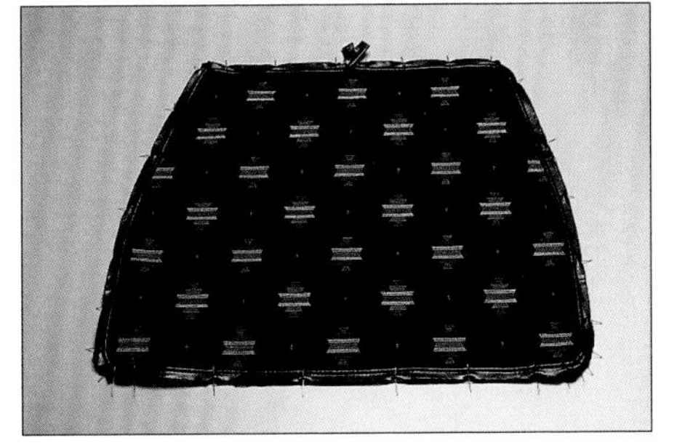

Starting at the center-back of the cushion top, pin piping on the right side of the fabric, matching the raw edge of the piping to the cut edge of the fabric. Check that the piping has a ½ in. (1.25 cm) seam allowance. If not, compensate. Pin well. At corners, clip into the seam allowance of the piping, allowing it to bend. At the start and the end, allow 2 in. (5 cm) extra piping, laying the ends across the seam allowance.

Attach the piping foot to the sewing machine. With matching thread, begin at the center-back and sew the piping in place, ½ in. (1.25 cm) from the cut edge.

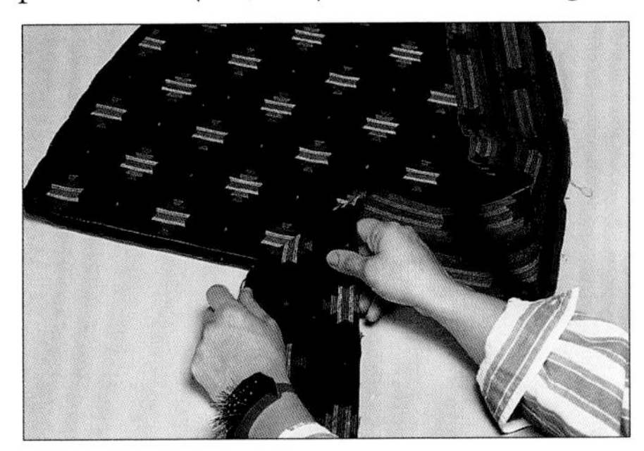

Lay a cut strip of fabric onto the piped edge of the cushion, with right sides together, matching the pattern along the front edge of the cushion. The ends of the strip should join at the center back. Pin the strip to the cushion top, starting at the center-front and working out, until the strip is pinned to the full perimeter of the cushion top. Clip the seam allowance of the strip at corners, if necessary. If the strip is too short, sew an additional section to the strip.

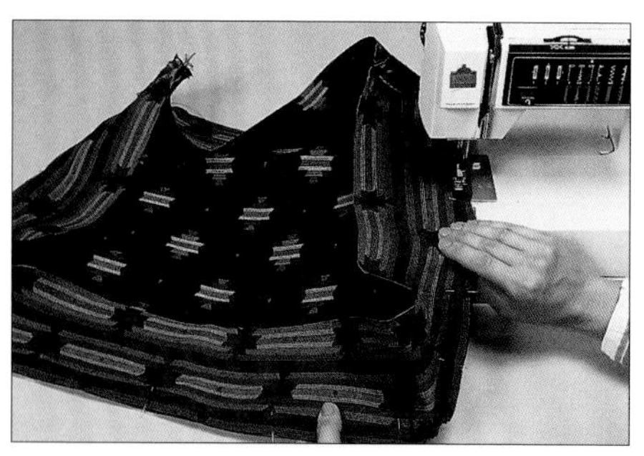

With the piping foot still in place, sew the strip tightly against the piping. Join the ends of the strip. Turn the cushion cover right-side-out and inspect the seam. Resew any gaps.

5 *Batting*

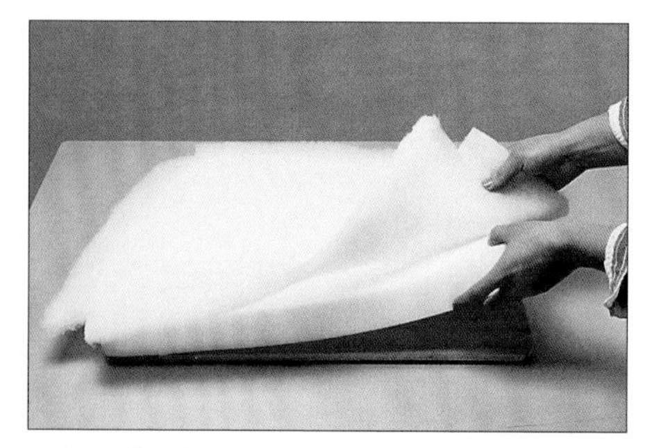

Using the foam as a guide, cut a piece of batting 3 in. (7.5 cm) larger all around (or measure and cut batting as shown on page 156, step 4). Lay the foam onto the plywood and the batting onto the foam. Notch the corners, so they dovetail when bent down over the sides of foam.

Optional: Gluing the foam to the plywood and the batting to the foam can reduce slippage. (See *Basic Seat Cushion*, steps 3 and 4, page 116.)

If you opt not to glue the plywood and the batting to the foam, lay the foam onto the rough side of the plywood and center the batting over the foam.

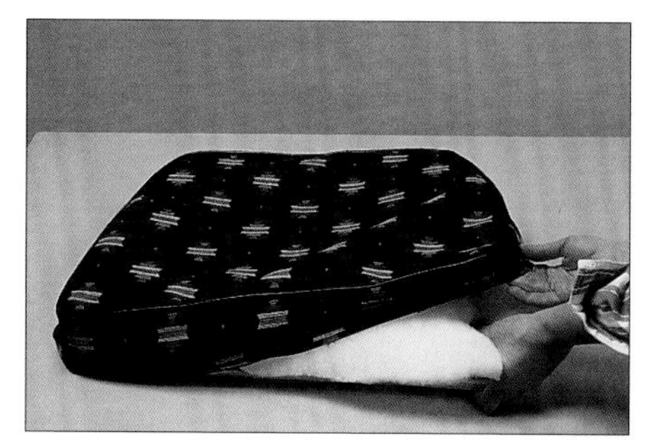

Slip the piped cushion top over the batting.

6 *Stapling*

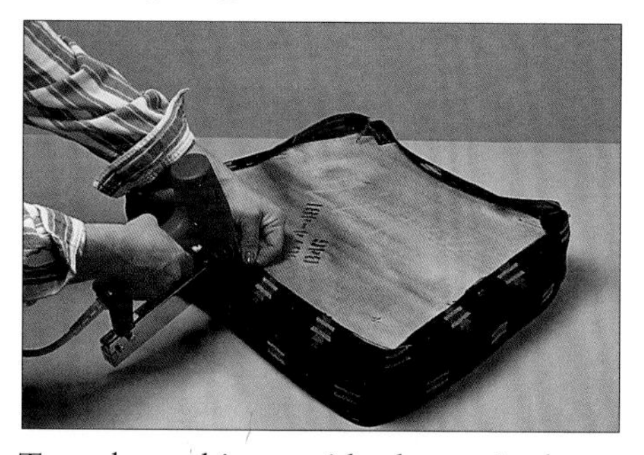

Turn the cushion upside-down. At the center of each side, gently but firmly pull the fabric to the back of the cushion and staple in place.

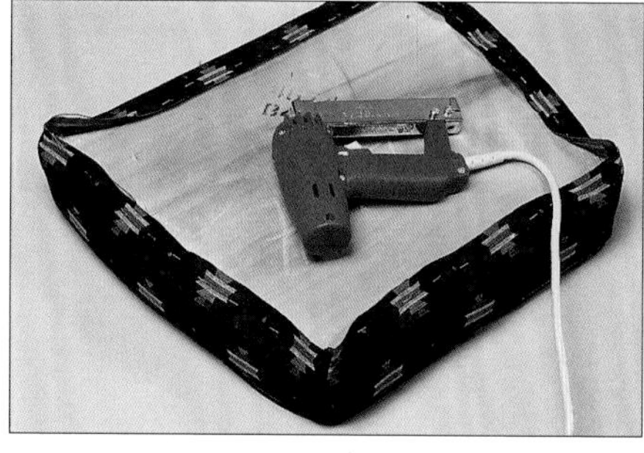

Continue, adding staples equally to all sides, keeping the tension even. Don't staple one full side before going on to the next. This will cause uneven tension and ripples.

Finish corners by stapling the center of the corner, then folding and stapling the excess down, like a fan, on both sides. Do several small folds to avoid puckering.

7 *Finishing*

Cut a piece of dust-cover cloth to fit the bottom of the cushion. It should cover the staples but be within the edge of the cushion. Staple it in place with one staple centered on each side. Work out from these staples, stapling all around the edge.

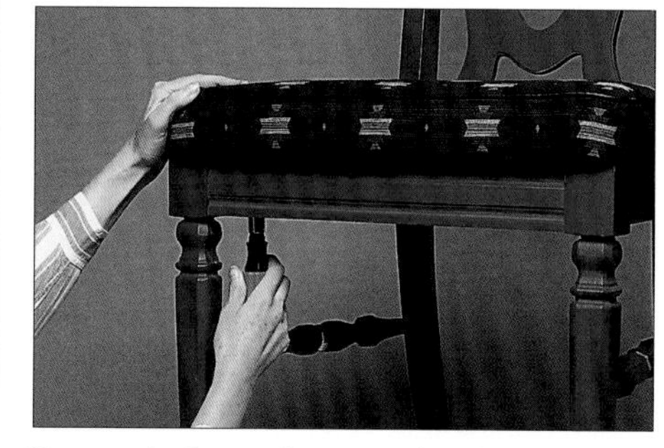

Reattach the cushion to the chair by screwing in appropriately sized screws from the bottom of the seat.

Woven Seat

Read This First

This technique is for replacing a worn-out webbing or split-cane seat. The seat must have the necessary dowel-like four rungs: front, back and sides. Purchase webbing at an upholstery supply store or buy wicking for oil lamps. The wicking shown here was bought at a hardware store in a 25 yard (23 m) roll for a surprisingly modest price. The wicking is a flatly woven natural cotton of a pleasing width. But why stop here? Many cast-off items can be used to great effect. Layers of ribbon, bunched yarn, or ends of trims can be used. Torn rags, tied end to end, could give a folksy, rag-rug feeling to a seat. Once started, stick to this project until finished (it only takes a few hours), so you won't lose track of the weaving.

MATERIALS

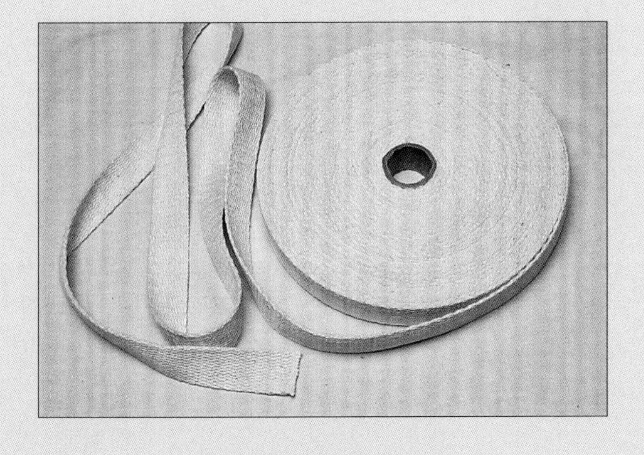

- approx. 20 yd. (20 m) wicking (the type used for oil lamps) or webbing about 1 in. (2.5 cm) wide (amount required can vary, depending on size of chair seat)
- stiff cardboard, 3 x 6 in. (7.5 x 15 cm)
- ruler and marker
- stir stick or other narrow stick, to fit the width of the seat
- white carpenter's glue and tape, or stapler and ¼ in. (.5 cm) staples
- *optional:* needle and thread for sewing webbing ends

1 *Getting started*

Cut a rectangle of stiff cardboard, about 3 x 6 in. (7.5 x 15 cm). Wrap the webbing around the length of the cardboard from end to end to make a shuttle. Don't cut the webbing.

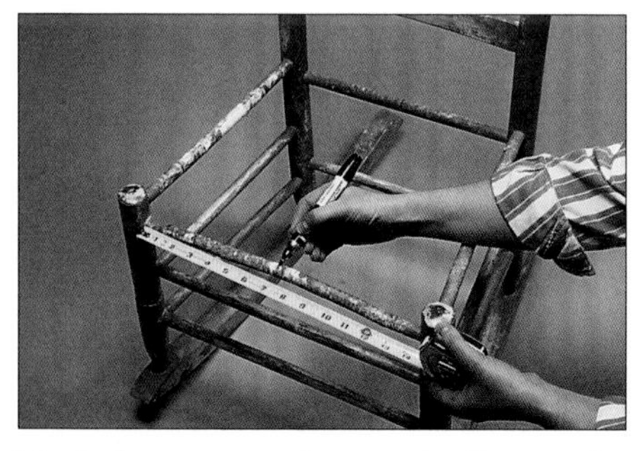

Mark the center points on the front and back rungs of the seat. The markings will help you keep the weaving straight, especially if the rungs are different lengths.

2 *The first pass*

Stand in front, facing the chair. Begin on the left side. Glue and tape (or staple) the webbing to the left-side rung. (Glue, tape and staples will be hidden by the weaving.)

Slip the shuttle under the back rung, then bring it up and over the back rung and toward the front, keeping the webbing flat.

Bring the shuttle forward, passing over the front rung, then under the chair seat to the back, and over the back rung again.

Keep the webbing even, neat and tight.

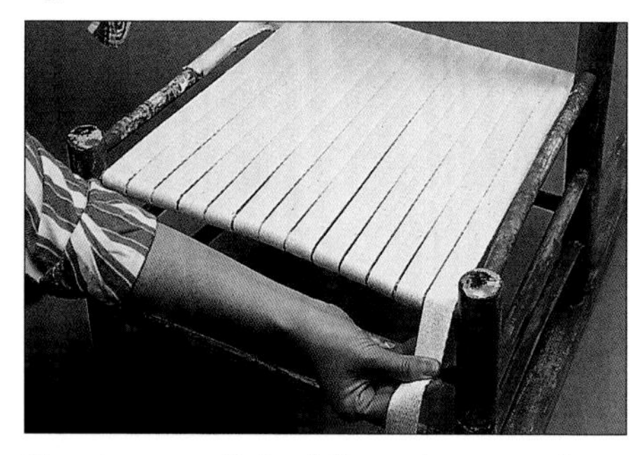

Continue until the full seat is covered, ending on top at the front right corner.

3 *Weaving*

Slip the shuttle under the seat to the back right. Bring it up, over the back rung, then under the right-side rung.

Weave the first row by bringing the shuttle over the right rung. Pass it *over the first strip* of webbing and under the second. Continue this over-under motion across the full width.

Using a ruler (or stir stick, as shown here), prop up the alternating strips under which you will pass. When you finish a row, remove the stick and reposition it for the next row. This will make the weaving easier and help you to avoid errors.

Turn the chair upside-down and weave across the back of the seat, as you did for the front.

Turn the chair right-side-up again. Reposition the ruler or stick. Weave the second row by bringing the shuttle up over the right-side rung. Pass the shuttle *under the first strip* and over the second. Then continue across the full width of the seat.

4 *Weaving, continued*

Continue in this manner, alternating the over-under weaving pattern. Stop to check the pattern occasionally. Keep the weaving tight by pushing it together with the tip of the ruler or stick.

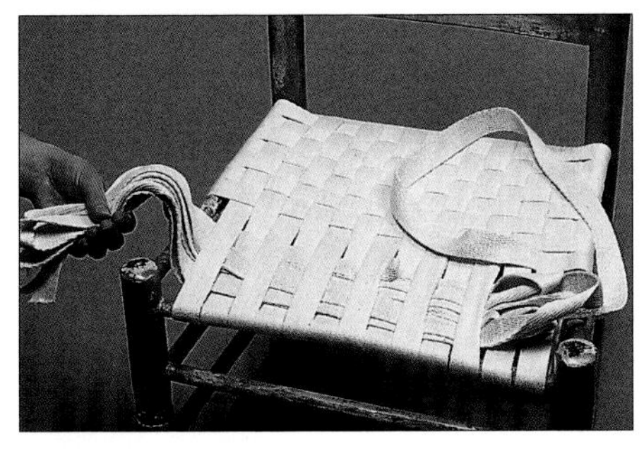

About halfway through the weaving, the shuttle may not fit through between the webbing. Take the webbing off the shuttle and pull it through in a loosely gathered bunch.

If the webbing isn't long enough and you need to join it, sew the ends together on the underside of the seat and tuck in any loose ends.

5 *Finishing*

Weave to the last row.

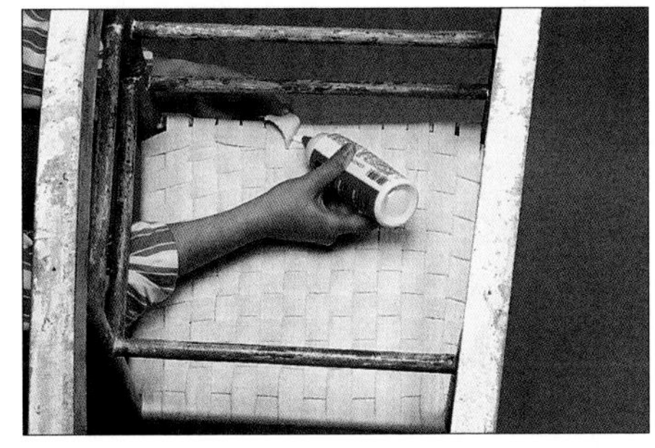

On the underside, weave halfway across the last row. Then cut the webbing and glue (or sew) the end down, tucking away any excess.

Backrest Cushions

Read This First

The decision to have a tailored or a shirred cushion on the seat's backrest is based on the style of the chair. A tailored cushion doesn't stand out. It is an integral part of the design of the chair. A shirred cushion, in contrast, commands attention. It makes a statement, giving the chair a showy, fashion-conscious sensibility. A tailored backrest cushion can be made from any type of fabric. A shirred backrest should be made from lightweight, finely woven fabric. The backrest can be finished decoratively with braid trim on the back side to hide staples, or by carefully gluing the finishing panel in place for a clean, crisp look.

MATERIALS

- plywood, ½ in. (1.25 cm) thick, good one side, to fit chair back (If the backrest is curved, reserve plywood from existing cushion.)
- high-density upholstery foam, 1 in. (2.5 cm) thick, cut to match the shape of the plywood
- fabric (To determine yardage, see step 2.)
- tape measure
- batting, 4 in. (10 cm) larger than the plywood both in length and in width
- stapler and ⅜ in. (1 cm) staples
- *for shirred cushion:* needle and thread
- hot-glue gun
- *for trimmed back:* 2 yd. (2 m) braid trim, 2 small pieces of tape
- dressmaker's pins
- screws (to reattach seat to chair), screwdriver
- small amount of paint to match fabric (for heads of screws)
- utility knife or X-acto knife
- *optional:* spray glue; scrap paper or dropsheet

1 *Getting started*

For all cushions: Remove the fabric and foam from the underlying plywood. Clean the plywood as thoroughly as possible, removing any mold and staples.

Have a piece of high-density upholstery foam, 1 in. (2.5 cm) thick, cut to match the size and shape of the plywood. Although it is best to have the foam professionally cut, foam this thin can be cut with scissors.

2 *Cutting fabric*

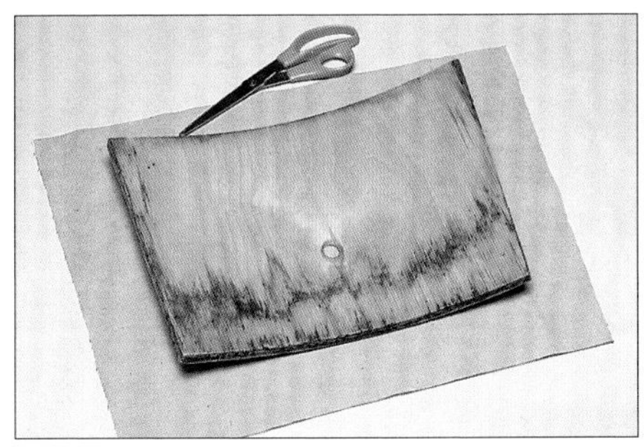

For tailored cushions: Lay the foam (or the plywood) onto the wrong side of the fabric. If the design printed on the fabric is directional (vines climbing a wall, for example), it should run up, from bottom of backrest to top. Measure and mark a cutting line 3 in. (7.5 cm) from the foam. Do this around the full perimeter. Cut along the line.

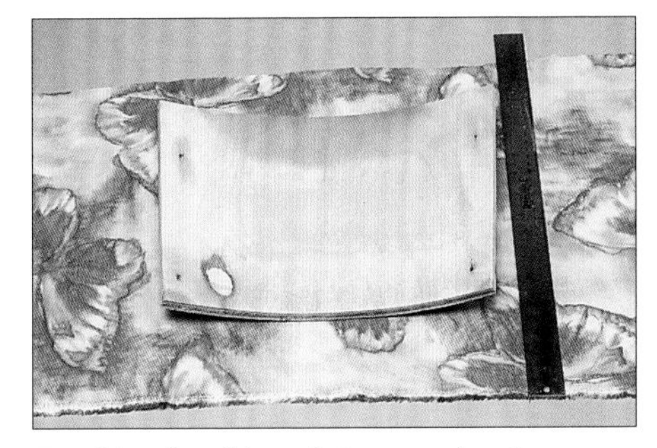

For shirred cushions: Measure the deepest section of the plywood backrest. Add 5 in. (12.5 cm). Cut fabric to this depth and to double the width of the backrest. Set the fabric aside.

For all cushions: Cut a piece of fabric 1 in. (2.5 cm) larger on all sides than the foam. This will be used to cover the back of the backrest cushion. If the design printed on the fabric is directional (vines climbing a wall, for example), it should run up, from bottom of backrest to top. Set the fabric aside.

3 *Cutting batting, gluing foam*

For all cushions: Cut batting 1½ in. (4 cm) larger on all sides than the foam. Notch the corners of the batting so that they dovetail when the batting is folded over the sides of the foam. Set the batting aside.

Optional: Gluing the foam to the plywood can reduce slippage. Lay down some scrap paper or a dropsheet and place the foam onto it. Check the directions on the spray-glue label for making a permanent bond. Spray the foam with glue.

Lay the gluey side of the foam onto the front side of the plywood.

4 *Gluing batting*

For all cushions. Optional: Lay the plywood and foam, foam-side-down, onto the batting. Using the spray glue, spray a section of the overhanging batting and fold the glued section up onto the side of the foam and plywood. Repeat until the batting is glued to the edges of the foam all the way around.

5 *Shirring*

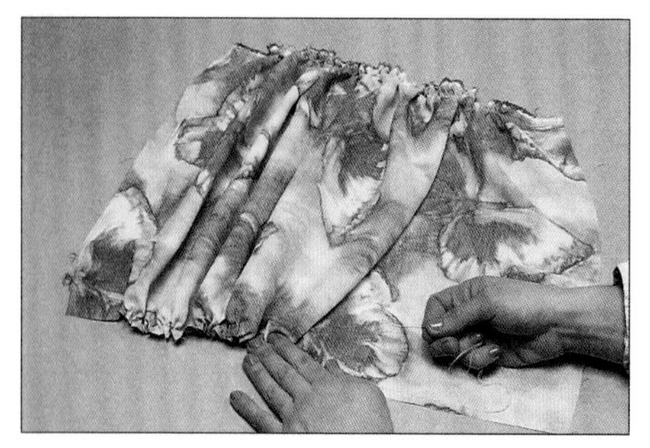

For shirred cushions: By machine or by hand, sew along the top and bottom edges of the fabric and gather to the width of the seat back, plus 5 in. (12.5 cm).

6 *Stapling*

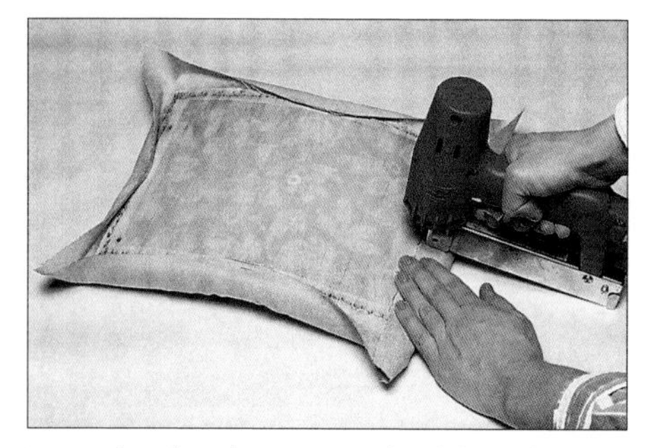

For tailored cushions: Lay the fabric face-down. Center the plywood/foam/batting section, batting-side-down, onto the wrong side of the fabric. Gently but firmly, pull the fabric onto the plywood and attach with one staple centered on each side.

7 *Stapling, continued*

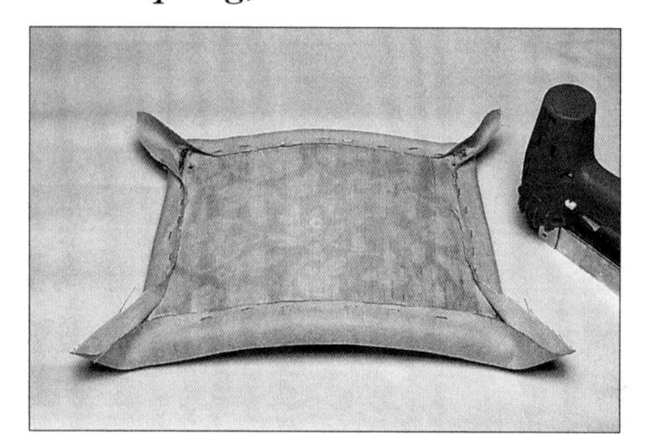

For tailored cushions: Work around the cushion, adding staples equally on all sides. Keep the pressure even.

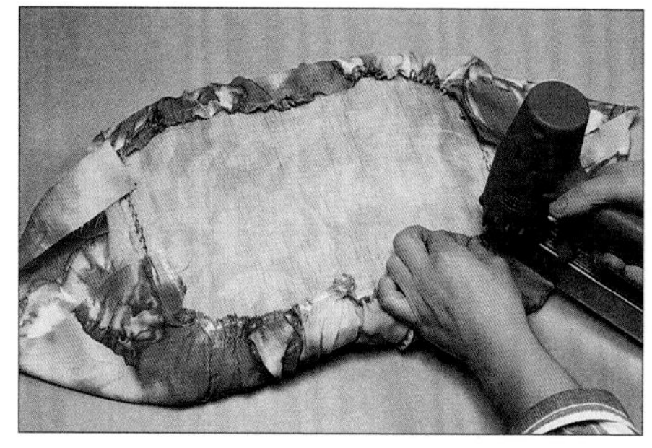

For shirred cushions: Don't staple the fabric at the sides yet, only at the top and bottom.

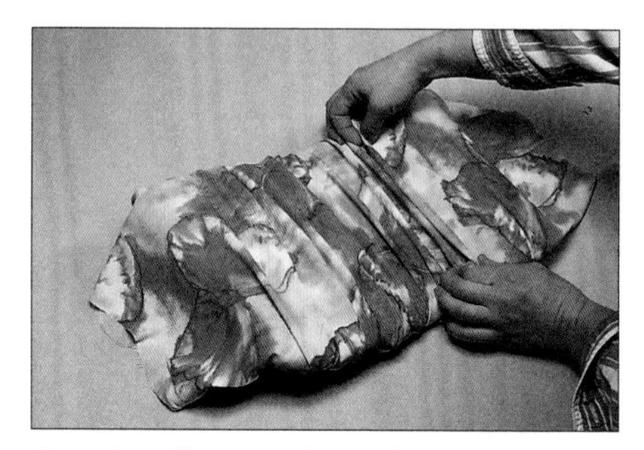

Occasionally turn the cushion to the front side and organize the gathers.

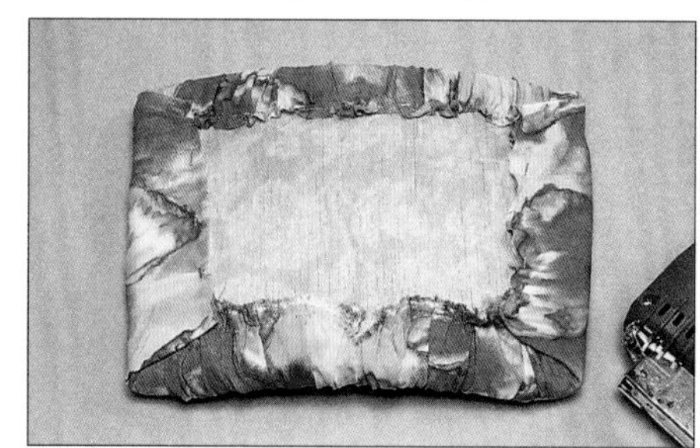

Staple the sides, with the fabric pulled taut. Pulling the fabric too tightly will disturb the gathers.

8 *Corners*

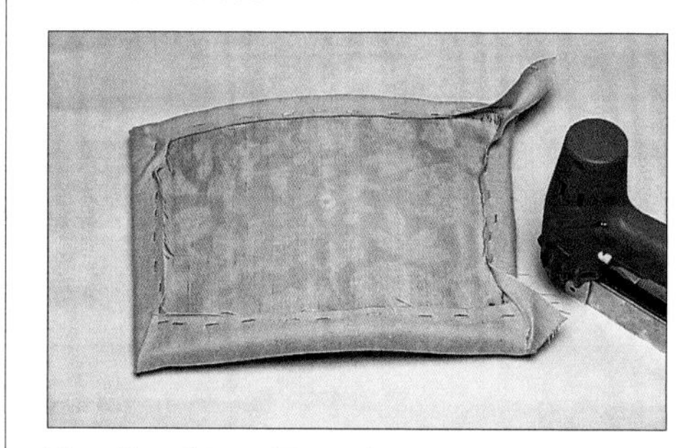

For all cushions: To make a neat corner, cut the point off the corner. Tuck one point into the overlap. Then fold the remaining point under. Staple in place.

9 *Finishing*

For all cushions: Find the fabric set aside for covering the back of the cushion. Fold and press the edges 2 in. (5 cm) to the wrong side.

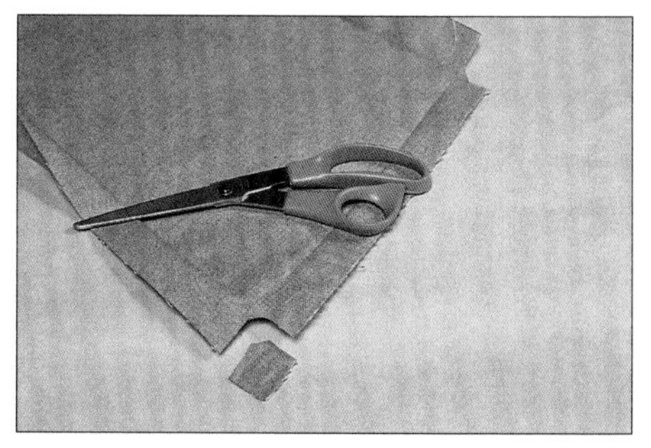

To make a neat corner, notch the corner nearly to the crease. Fold one edge flat. Then fold the other edge over it, tucking the corner under.

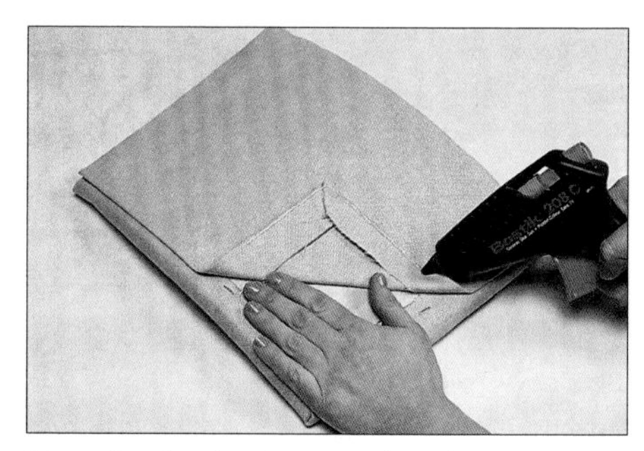

For a flat finish: Heat up the glue gun. *Be careful not to burn your fingers, especially if you are not experienced with a glue gun.* The glue becomes hot enough to cause deep burns, and the glue sticks and keeps burning.

Position the fabric, centered onto the back of the cushion, right-side-up. Pin at the corners. Unpin and lift one corner. With the glue gun at high heat, squeeze a narrow, neat bead just inside the folded edge of the fabric. Lay the corner down, allow the glue to cool and lift the next

corner. Repeat until the back is glued on all the way around.

10 *Finishing, continued*

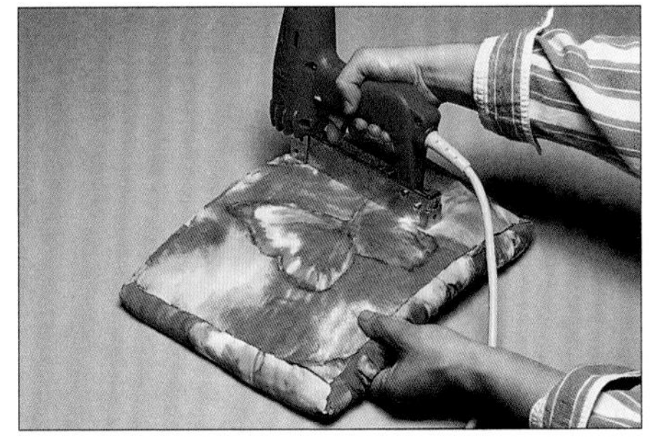

For a trimmed finish: Plug in the glue gun. Lay the fabric centered onto the back of the cushion, right-side-up. Staple the fabric to the back of the cushion, centering one staple on each of the four sides. Staples must be carefully placed at the edge of the fold of the fabric. Otherwise, they will not be covered by the trim. Work out from the positioning staples equally, stapling along the edges of the fabric on all four sides.

Wrap a small piece of tape around the end of the braid to prevent fraying. Carefully apply hot glue to the taped end of the braid, then slip this end under the edge of the fabric between two staples, hiding the tape. Working in sections, apply a bead of hot glue to the underside of the braid and lay the braid glue-side-down, hiding the staples and the folded edge of the fabric.

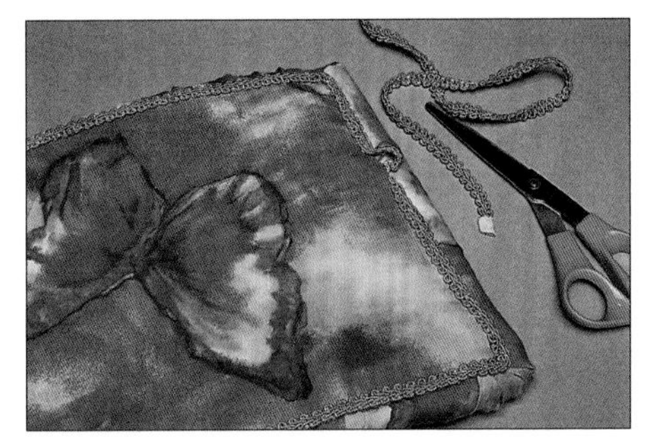

When the braid is glued on all the way around, cut it with 1 in. (2.5 cm) excess. Tape around the end. Apply glue to the end and tuck it into the gap with the other end, keeping the join as invisible as possible.

11 *Reattaching cushions*

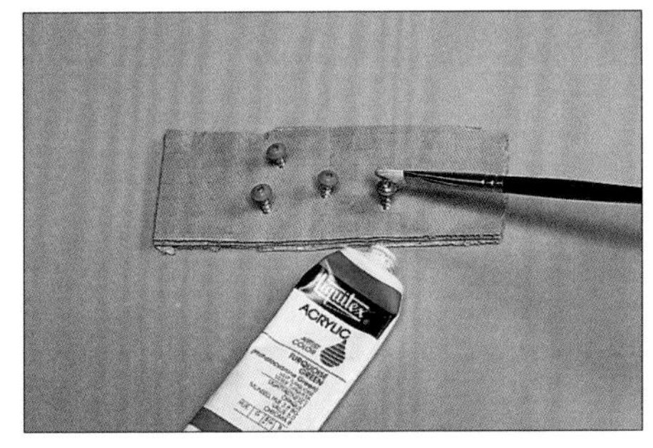

For all cushions: In a color compatible with the fabric, paint the heads of the screws to be used for reattaching the seat.

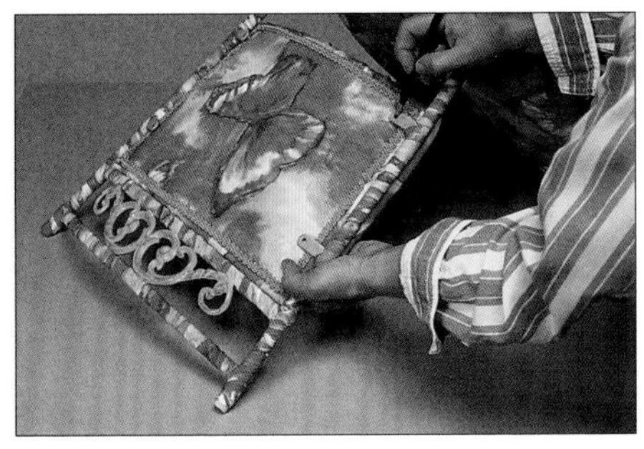

Position the seat back into the chair. Mark where the screw holes will go.

Using a sharp utility knife or X-acto knife, cut a tiny hole at each of the marks. The cut should break only one or two threads, allowing the screws to pass through the fabric. If these holes are not cut, the fabric will bunch when the screws are screwed in.

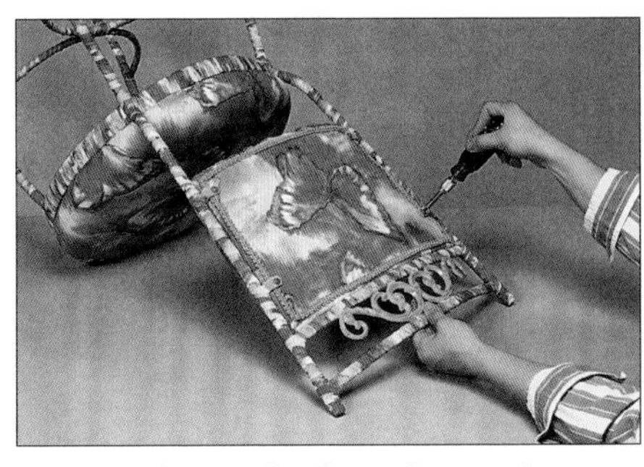

Position the seat back in place and screw in the screws.

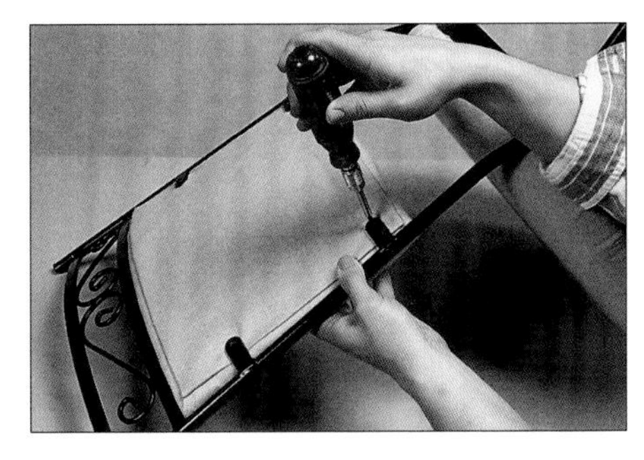

Joy von Tiedemann

SHEILA MCGRAW began her career painting sets and designing props for major high-fashion retailers. She then moved into the highly competitive world of freelance illustration, producing art for newspapers, magazines, advertising and package design. Next she turned to illustrating children's books. Her first book, Robert Munsch's *Love You Forever,* became an international bestseller that reached number one on the *New York Times* Children's Bestseller List.

An avid home sewer, decorator and painter, she has written numerous craft books, including *Papier-Mâché for Kids,* a bestseller that won the prestigious Benjamin Franklin Award. Her books on painted and decorated furniture have firmly established her as one of the foremost writers in the field. Sheila McGraw lives on a farm north of Toronto and is the mother of three grown sons.

Books Written By Sheila McGraw

Papier-Mâché Today; Papier-Mâché for Kids; Soft Toys to Sew; Gifts Kids Can Make; Dolls Kids Can Make; Pussycats Everywhere; This Old New House; Painting and Decorating Furniture; Decorating Furniture: Antique and Country Paint Projects; Decorating Furniture: Découpage, Paint and Fabric Projects; Decorating Furniture: Stencil, Paint and Block Print Projects; Decorating Furniture: Texture, Paint, Ornament and Mosaic Projects

Books Illustrated By Sheila McGraw

Love You Forever, I Promise I'll Find You, Lightning Bug Thunder